Keri Kitay is a communications professional who has a passion for health and wellbeing. Having witnessed the devastating impact Alzheimer's can have on a person, she feels it is her duty and responsibility to educate people and provide tools to assist others to make better-informed health decisions.

Keri is also a sister, daughter, granddaughter, aunty, friend and colleague who believes in the welfare of others. She is an ambassador for the Centre for Healthy Brain Ageing (CHeBA) and has been a board member for the United Israel Appeal (UIA).

THE LONG GOODBYE

Keri Kitay

 hachette
AUSTRALIA

IMPORTANT NOTE TO READERS: This book details the personal experiences of the author and must not be treated as a substitute for qualified medical advice. Always consult a qualified medical practitioner. Neither the author nor the publisher can be held responsible for any loss or claim arising out of the use, or misuse, of the suggestions made or the failure to take professional advice.

hachette
AUSTRALIA

Published in Australia and New Zealand in 2024
by Hachette Australia
(an imprint of Hachette Australia Pty Limited)
Gadigal Country, Level 17, 207 Kent Street, Sydney, NSW 2000
www.hachette.com.au

The authorised representative
in the EEA is
Hachette Ireland
8 Castlecourt Centre
Dublin 15, D15 XTP3, Ireland
(email: info@hbgi.ie)

Hachette Australia acknowledges and pays our respects to the past, present and future Traditional Owners and Custodians of Country throughout Australia and recognises the continuation of cultural, spiritual and educational practices of Aboriginal and Torres Strait Islander peoples. Our head office is located on the lands of the Gadigal people of the Eora Nation.

A catalogue record for this book is available from the National Library of Australia

ISBN: 978 0 7336 5128 1 (paperback)

Cover design by Adam Williams
Cover art by Terry Kitay, courtesy of the Kitay family
Author photograph courtesy of Tali Gordon
Typeset in 12/20pt Sabon LT Std by Kirby Jones
Printed and bound in Great Britain by Clays Ltd, Elcograf S.p.A.

To Mom, Dad, Ricky and Greg,
without you, I would not be me.
Thank you for allowing me to share our story,
and for your unwavering support.

A NOTE ON THE BOOK COVER

Mom wasn't what you would refer to as an artist but it was always clear that she could draw and did possess some artistic flair. I can't recall exactly why we decided to have Kelly come and paint with Mom. Perhaps it was because Dad knew Mom could paint or we were advised that it might be a good activity for Mom to do. When Mom painted with Kelly, there was an ease about her. Whether she knew what she was setting out to paint or not, Mom created several pieces of art during the time that she had Alzheimer's. When Dad would come home, she would show him her work with pride and joy and when we saw it we would always praise Mom for what she had created.

There was one painting in particular which Mom created with Kelly that turned out to be a beautifully messy work of great artistic merit. In some way, it seemed to be a representation of her life at the time: beautiful and colourful moments interjected with sadness, confusion and uncertainty. When Mom passed away, we framed this piece of art and it has been hanging in my brother Greg's home ever since.

When it came to deciding what the cover of this book would be, it was important that my family and I had a personal connection to the cover. In conversations about what the cover should be, my sister-in-law mentioned the painting and took a screenshot and sent it to me. When I mocked-up a cover that featured the art, I felt an immediate connection. This was it.

The painting by Terry Kitay used on the cover of this book is a true representation of the arduous battle Mom faced throughout her Alzheimer's journey and a reminder of the beautiful moments that she was able to experience amid it all. It's a reminder that even within the darkest of times, there will be moments of colour and joy, and that these conflicting emotions can be experienced simultaneously. It's a reminder that Mom's light and presence in our family's lives will never fade.

CONTENTS

INTRODUCTION

It can be easy to romanticise the kind of life you want to live. To imagine a future filled with fun, adventure, success and happiness. But real life isn't a fairytale, and happy endings aren't guaranteed. So it's important to find fulfilment and create meaning, no matter how your life pans out. When I think about what that means, I am drawn to the notion of legacy, of how I will be remembered by the loved ones I leave behind. My hope is that I will be remembered for how I made people feel, for how I served others, and for the impact I made on the world. I think about this a lot. Everything I do needs to mean something – it always comes back to purpose. Our time on this earth is more about what we can do for others than what we can do for ourselves.

When I first felt the urge to write about the impact of Alzheimer's disease on my family, I knew that I couldn't ignore it. It felt like a calling. In 2010, our world changed forever. We didn't know it then, but that was the beginning of an almost ten-year journey that has shaped me in ways I never thought possible. It was the start of a life I'd never envisaged for myself or my family.

As I transferred my thoughts into words, I relived pain, anger, confusion, sadness and frustration. But among those feelings, the thing that stood out the most was how cathartic writing was. I could collect my thoughts, put them down, and once I'd released them, feel a sense of relief. Like I'd been freed from the experiences I was describing.

The more I wrote, the clearer my reason for writing became. In part, I was doing it to share my feelings about everything my family and I had been through. But also, I would read over what I had written and think if only I'd had these notes or something like them in the early days, how helpful that would have been. If I'd had a resource that helped me navigate the situation, validate what was happening, what I was feeling and shown me what to expect, what a difference that might have made.

So I knew I had to keep writing, because one day this would become a resource I could share with the world, in the hope it would help anyone in a similar situation – those dealing with dementia, which is a general term for cognitive decline, or more specifically Alzheimer's, which is the brain disease that accounts for around three-quarters of dementia cases. More than anything, I wanted to help advocate for people with Alzheimer's and their families, to educate the world on how to treat them, and to eradicate the stigma around Alzheimer's and other forms of dementia.

Admittedly, before my mother – 'Mom' to me and my family – was diagnosed with Alzheimer's, I knew very little about the disease, which is shocking because Alzheimer's is the second leading cause of death in Australia. Truthfully, I thought that it was an old person's disease where they just lost their memory. What a misconception that was. I learned quickly that Alzheimer's affects more than a person's memory. It impacts thinking and behaviours, and these symptoms get worse over time and impact daily life. And it can be fatal: I remember a friend from school whose dad developed dementia and passed away from complications. I was devastated for her, but little did I know how soon I would closely relate to her heartbreak.

Throughout the eight years during which Mom endured Alzheimer's, I felt completely helpless. There was simply nothing I could do to change the condition she had, and that feeling didn't sit well with me. I am a solutions-based person. In my work life, I live by the motto that there's always a way through, an answer to every problem.

But this was not a work problem; this was Mom's real life. So I started looking at what I could contribute, how I could make some kind of difference. If I could not help Mom directly, then surely there was some other way I could have an impact.

This book is my opportunity to honour Mom and everything she endured, so that others, including the next generation, are better equipped to deal with Alzheimer's. My story has been written to inform people about what they may go through, and help guide them through it. My hope is that it will resonate with and provide comfort to many, and that if people ever find themselves in a similar situation, it is met with empathy and kindness.

I speak a lot about resilience: in everyday conversations, at the fundraising events I host, in all my professional endeavours. It's a daily topic of conversation, especially when you run your own business. You encounter extreme highs and lows, incredible wins and disappointing losses, but you learn to get up and move forward. Life has thrown me some pretty big curveballs since Mom started showing visible signs of Alzheimer's in 2010. It has certainly challenged my one-time idyllic picture of life. But I truly believe that how we respond to challenges is what defines us. We don't always get things right, but acknowledging that and learning from our mistakes is important, to make sure that next time we do better.

When I think about Mom's legacy, it's not her Alzheimer's that comes to mind. I think about kindness, her empathy, her love and devotion to our family, her willingness to put everyone else first, her values and morals, the way she treated everyone with respect. I think about the way she made people feel, her lifelong service to others, her decency and honesty. This is Mom's legacy.

My hopes in writing this book are to honour that legacy, and to empower advocates for people with dementia and other disabilities or diseases, so that they may be able to better support their loved ones, give them a voice when they can't speak for themselves, and ensure they are always respected and remembered.

The final moments of Mom's life were so profound for me and my family, and my thoughts from that time have informed this book. But the journey as a whole has influenced how I live my life and approach my health, including making choices that will enable me to live a long time. I will do everything in my power to prevent or delay the development of Alzheimer's. It is my duty to intentionally care about my health and that of those around me.

When I was twelve, my parents made the ultimate sacrifice in deciding to leave South Africa to emigrate to Australia in order to give my brothers and I the best chance at a good life and I am eternally grateful to them. So when

Mom was diagnosed with Alzheimer's, although nothing could have prepared us for what lay ahead, giving Mom the best care possible was the least we could do.

It was life-changing and rocked our world in unimaginable ways, however the life lessons we learned truly have given this whole experience meaning.

Mom used to say that I was a 'closed book', so it's somewhat ironic that here I am baring all to the world. It's not as though I don't like to talk to anyone, it's just that I'd rather listen to other people and help them. Also, for most of my life, there were no real issues to discuss. But this book, and this story, are so much bigger than me, and I intend to use them to advocate for the next person who is diagnosed with Alzheimer's, and their family. I don't regret not being that open throughout life with Mom, or anyone else for that matter. I'm not the person who is going to shower you with hugs and affection. I won't tell you constantly that I love you. But I will always show up for you as a friend, daughter, sister, aunty and person. I believe that actions speak volumes.

I am immensely grateful for the traits I inherited from Mom. She was the most selfless person in the world. She devoted her life to Dad, my brothers and me, asking nothing in return. Mom's story is a constant reminder that what sets us apart in the world is how we serve others and our desire to leave the world a better place.

Chapter 1

KOL NIDREI

It was 8 October 2019 – Kol Nidrei night. In the Jewish religion, this marks the beginning of the holiest day of the year, Yom Kippur (the day of atonement), itself the start of a 25-hour fast where we repent for our sins and ask for forgiveness. In the days leading up to Kol Nidrei, Mom had started to slip away. She'd refrained from eating and her breathing had become heavier, and even though something similar had happened only six months earlier, this time felt different. We spent hours sitting at her bedside holding her hand and listening as her heavy breathing turned to rasping.

On that Kol Nidrei night, Mom – or Terry to those outside the family – passed away in Sydney from early-onset Alzheimer's after an arduous eight-year battle.

She took her last breaths surrounded by people who loved her. There was my dad – Martin, her husband – and her three children: my older brother Greg and younger brother Ricky, and me. You hear about the moment when someone passes as being significant, that the person passing has waited for just the right time to slip away. But until you experience it first-hand, you can never truly understand the profound impact of that moment.

Before Mom became unwell, every year on Kol Nidrei my family went to the synagogue. But when she wasn't able to go anymore, I too stopped going – I would sit with her at home, and later in the nursing home. I just didn't enjoy going to the synagogue without her. Jewish holidays are about family, and as men and women sit separately, I had no desire to sit alone. This worked out well for my brothers, as I would also be available to babysit their kids so they could go to the synagogue. On that night in 2019, I was babysitting my niece at Ricky's house when I got a call from Dad. On leaving the synagogue, he'd been contacted by the home where Mom was living and told that the family needed to come straightaway, as things were not looking good. He'd then called me and contacted Greg, and as soon as Ricky came home, we all rushed there together. It was around 9.30 p.m. and the home was only a few streets away.

Without saying a word to one another, we all knew in our hearts that this would be the last time we would be with Mom. We went straight to her room, where she was lying in bed, breathing hard. The four of us sat around her and just held her hand, stared at her, and in silence spent the most meaningful hours beside her. My family had always expected openness about my mom's situation; we'd never wanted anyone to sugar-coat what was going on, as we knew that her condition was degenerative and all we had was limited time. So when we asked the nurse what he thought would happen, he said without hesitation that she would pass in the next twelve hours. We decided at that point to go home and get some sleep, then come back in the morning. Each of us, in our own time and our own way, said our goodbyes. We gave each other the space to hold her, to kiss her head one last time.

Walking out of the home, I didn't really know what to feel. I had somewhat of a heavy heart, yet at the same time I breathed a sigh of relief.

While he was walking home, Greg wrote some notes in his phone about the experience, about how he felt about it being the final goodbye. Without knowing this at the time, when I got home, I too wrote notes on my phone to capture what I'd just experienced.

What a surreal moment. Sitting and literally watching someone take some of their last breaths, giving them permission to let go. I've always believed that a person will stop fighting to live when they are at peace with their surroundings. Over the past forty-eight hours my mom has had her children and husband sitting around her like the matriarch that she is, her three brothers and family putting all our differences aside because the thing we have in common is our love for Mom, wife and sister. Now that she has seen that, that she has gotten us all together, she can leave peacefully. She was always the peace-maker. She stood up for all of us and she united us. She continues to do that without the ability to speak, but her presence, her strong will and love for her family binds us together.

To love someone so much that you are willing to let them go for their own peace is the ultimate sacrifice, but one that needs to be made.

I don't know when I wake up tomorrow if she will still be gasping for air, but I do know her brightness, her light and her presence will live on inside and around all of us forever. Go in peace Mom. I love you.

Thirty minutes after leaving the home, we received a call saying that Mom had passed.

* * *

Earlier, the five of us sitting together in peace and harmony at the home would have been the ultimate moment for Mom. She would have taken her last breath knowing we were united, and could then let us go. For it to happen on that significant day of the Jewish calendar evokes my mother: a beautiful soul who gave so much, so effortlessly and selflessly.

I felt numb with shock, even though I had said my goodbye and made peace with it. I was aware that, since Mom had gone to live in a care home, we'd been going to visit her every week – more frequently when she'd moved to another home closer to us – but now we would no longer be seeing her. That part of our lives had ended.

It is customary in the Jewish religion that, after someone passes, the body not be left alone until the funeral. Mom was covered by a sheet, and my brothers, my dad and I sat together in her room, joined later by Mom's two brothers who also lived in Sydney. We sat peacefully, we cried, and at the same time we experienced a sense of relief: Mom was now at rest, she was free, and so were we.

It is also customary when a Jewish person passes to contact the Chevra Kadisha, an organisation of Jewish men and women who ensure that the bodies of deceased Jews are prepared for burial according to Jewish customs. Usually they would come straightaway and collect the deceased, but as it was Yom Kippur, the holy Jewish day which involves a twenty-five-hour fast solely focused on atonement and repentance, the Chevra Kadisha contact number diverted to a funeral home. We were also required to have a doctor prepare a medical certificate identifying the cause of death. We stayed in the room until the funeral home people came and took her – someone from the funeral home would stay with Mom's body until Yom Kippur ended the following evening.

It was a strange feeling, watching her body being taken away; we all felt a little lost, unsure of what to do next. I didn't think I would be able to sleep that night, but the shock of the moment and memories of the past eight years gave way to sheer exhaustion, and back home I passed out.

Everything felt strange when I woke up the following morning. Had it all been a dream? And then reality hit, and I felt lost again. I went over to Greg's house, and because we were fasting I couldn't even make myself so much as a cup of tea. Dad and the boys decided they would go to the synagogue, as on Yom Kippur you say Yizkor – the mourner's prayer. This prayer is said only by those who have lost someone in their immediate family, and everyone else goes outside during this time. Ironically, it had always been Mom who would stay in the synagogue for Yizkor, as she had lost both her parents; the rest of us would always leave. Not so now.

I didn't go to the synagogue myself, instead staying at my brother's house and just lying on the couch. I have no recollection of what I did in those hours. I do know that most of us use Yom Kippur to disconnect, refraining from using our phones, so I didn't contact anyone to let them know what had happened. But later, two of my oldest friends, Ashlyn and Carli, arrived at my brother's house, having learned at the synagogue about Mom passing, and I couldn't have felt more comforted. We had been friends since primary school in South Africa, growing up in each other's homes, and they knew the warm woman who was my mom. They had eaten her famous bran muffins. Ashlyn and I had shared birthday parties, and Carli had thrown my farewell party when I'd emigrated to Australia, a few years before their own families emigrated too. We had created a lifetime of memories together. So it was calming to be able to talk about Mom and remember the good old days – I was so grateful for them being there.

Still, most of that day is a blur: sometimes I just stared at nothing, oblivious, while at other times I thought deeply about what had transpired the night before. What did it all mean? How had the last eight years culminated in this moment? They'd been eight years of watching the most important person in my life slowly slip away, losing a piece of herself every so often, not being able to do the normal things that we take for granted every day. She'd gone from being a capable, happy mother, wife, sister and friend, to a person withdrawn and unable to look after herself, as if her soul had been taken out of her. So much

13

of her became trapped and lost to Alzheimer's that, when I think back, it's often hard to remember what Mom was like before all that. But inevitably I do remember, and it's as clear as day. She was the most positive person, someone who would do anything for anyone. She was the mother who came to watch every sporting match, driving my brothers and me all over the place. She took us to school and picked us up every day. She always had a snack waiting for us. If we needed anything, she was literally just a phone call away. She was my shopping partner, my biggest fan. She was also an avid dancer, tennis player and social butterfly. She was fortunate to live a beautiful life where she could have anything she wanted, but she never wanted much because she had her family, and that was all she needed.

Alzheimer's leaves you feeling so helpless as an outsider, a feeling amplified by your love of those going through it. There is no cure. You research everything, speak to every professor, try to change the person's diet, try to start them on an exercise regime, but you can't stop or reverse the disease. You investigate every clinical trial but, as yet, there has been little in the way of promising results. So you feel powerless, vulnerable and inadequate. All you *can* do is make that person's journey as comfortable and as filled with love as possible, and dedicate as much time as possible to them. You don't know this at the start, though – it's certainly something I only learned much later on in Mom's journey.

The worst and best thing about Alzheimer's is you have no idea what the person is feeling, or how aware they are of what is going on. It's terrible to begin with, but later, as the disease takes hold, this unknown can give you a sense of comfort – that perhaps the person is shielded from what's happening. Of course, all of that is quickly dismissed when they have a moment of lucidity, and you as a loved one feel a sense of hope. But that feeling of hope doesn't last long, nor do the moments of lucidity. Everyone finds comfort in their own way. My comfort, after a few years, was believing that Mom was completely unaware of what was going on – I'll never know if that was accurate or not.

In saying that, I do believe that Mom was aware when we were around her, that she may not have recognised who we were but she knew we belonged. She smiled the most when little children were around: her grandchildren, whom she never got to know properly. Somehow, when they were there, visiting her or playing in her garden, she beamed. Perhaps such moments of family transcend any disease.

Chapter 2

ESHET CHAYIL
(Woman of Valour)

I have two very different memories of Mom: pre-Alzheimer's and with Alzheimer's. When we were in the thick of it, it was hard to remember Mom before her diagnosis. It was as though that version of her had been blocked from my mind, as if Alzheimer's had reshaped my memory. Such is the devastating force of this type of dementia. It wasn't as though she was a stranger, more a shell of who she had once been. The reality of the present overshadowed memories of the past.

* * *

Mom was born on 13 July 1956 in Johannesburg, South Africa. She was the youngest of four, with three brothers. Her parents desperately wanted to have a girl, and after three boys they were sure the next would be a girl. When Mom was born and her parents' dream came true, they were elated – Mom was the apple of their eyes.

From an early age, it was evident that Mom loved being around people. She was so social, and loved to sleep over at her friends' and cousins' places. As a little girl, whenever it rained and thundered, she would be so scared she'd climb into bed with her eldest brother, seeking protection. Her brothers remained protective of Mom throughout her life.

The four kids would spend their weekends at the Jewish Guild, a sports club that their father attended every weekend, and where families would spend time together. Mom enjoyed swimming and playing with the other kids, true to her social nature. Her love of sport extended to netball, calling on her brothers to practise with her in the garden – they would always oblige. She also started dancing at a young age and was skilled at ballet and Spanish dancing. Her brothers watched so many of her dance performances, they knew all her dance moves. She was so good at Spanish dancing that at one point she was only one exam away from becoming a teacher, but then she suddenly gave it up – a mystery that Alzheimer's prevented us from ever solving.

Mom was very spoilt. Like her brothers, her dad would do anything for her. He built her a massive doll's house in the garden. It was the size of a real bedroom and was decked out with furniture. Mom spent whole days playing in it. Despite her pampered childhood, or perhaps because of it, Mom became a caring and selfless adult. When she was older, she spent her spare time volunteering at the Selwyn Segal, a Jewish care facility for people with physical and intellectual disabilities. She loved her time there, helping out and entertaining the residents.

Mom was volunteering at the Selwyn Segal care facility one day when Dad and a friend turned up. Their intentions were not as pure as Mom's, as they were there to 'pick up' Jewish chicks while fronting themselves as good Jewish men. Drawn in by Mom's beautiful smile and friendly nature, Dad must have turned on some serious charm to woo her. She was nineteen years old and he was twenty. On their first date, Dad arrived at Mom's home with flowers, but he was too nervous to give them to her in front of her brothers – it was only once they'd left that Dad handed Mom his gift.

Mom and Dad got married on 2 April 1978 at the Emmarentia Synagogue, with the ceremony followed by a dinner dance at the Simon Kuper Hall. Mom had a huge family, so when they celebrated Jewish festivals, they would hire out a hall to accommodate everyone. Her wedding was no different. Dad describes it as a massive affair, an elegant evening with lots of people, everyone having a great time. Dad wore a brown velvet suit, while Mom's wedding dress was elegant and understated, representative of who she was.

Not long after the wedding, Dad went into the army, which was compulsory for men in South Africa on reaching a certain age. The army base was only an hour from home, so some nights Mom would drive out there, pick up Dad and his best friend, take them out for the night and drop them back the following morning at 6 a.m. in time for their shifts. These younger years brought out a fun, spontaneous side to Mom, characteristics we'd eventually lose to Alzheimer's. Mom also joined the Jewish Women's Benevolent Society, an organisation that cared for elderly and indigent people. Mom always gave back to the community – it was innate.

Mom had her first child, my older brother Greg, when she was twenty-five years old, followed by me two years later and Ricky when she was thirty. She was the ultimate mother, with us being her pride and joy. I cannot recall a single time she shouted at me or my brothers. I remember her jokingly raising her voice at Dad, but never with malice, and no doubt only when he deserved it. Dad has a rather warped sense of humour, something he and I share – we are not always proud of it, but it has provided us with many laughs over the years. Mom did not share our sense of humour; she was too kind and gracious to ever talk out of line. When Dad and I exploded into fits of laughter over something a little crude, she would often give us a death stare so we knew she was not impressed. That was as grave as any punishment ever got.

Mom and Dad were very different in their approaches to parenting but remained a united front. She was the heart and soul of our home: softer, kinder and more compassionate. Mom may not have said a lot, but she didn't need to. Her values and morals set the tone of the house, and have been carried by us our entire lives. She taught us patience and kindness and *tzedakah* (charity). Dad, on the other hand, was more direct, always needing things to be done his way. He wasn't what I would call strict, just firmer in his parenting style.

Mom was famous for baking bran muffins, the smell of which almost always welcomed us kids home. In fact, everyone who came to our house would always be offered one. Mom loved being in the kitchen and baking. When it was anyone's birthday, she would be the one to make the birthday cake. She was possibly even more famous for her ice-cream recipe, and she would make rice crispy ice-cream on a Friday night for the Jewish Shabbat dinner, which always proved a huge hit with us kids.

She wrote down all her recipes, and it has now become a tradition for my best friend and me to bake her bran muffins on her birthday for the family:

Mom's bran muffins

Ingredients:

5 cups self-raising flour

300 grams raisin bran

2.5 cups brown sugar (sticky)

1 litre buttermilk

1 cup oil

5 teaspoons bicarb soda

Method:

Add all ingredients into a bowl and mix together

Pour into muffin baking trays

Bake in oven on 180°C for 20 minutes

* * *

There was one lifelong friend that Mom liked to share lots of recipes with: Mrs P. No-one knew Mom better. Mrs P and Mom were the best of friends, and our families spent so much time together in South Africa, on holiday and going over to each other's homes for a *braai* (barbecue). When Mom and Mrs P were together, it was truly something special. They celebrated each other's twenty-first birthdays, their weddings, and having kids – all of life's greatest milestones.

Reflecting fondly on her friendship with Mom, Mrs P says: 'Te [Terry] and I had a very special relationship for nearly sixty years. There were times over the years when you guys left [South Africa] we didn't speak or see each other as much, but we still had the most incredible connection. She was like a sister to me. We confided in one another, giggled and had such fun.'

When Mom met Dad, Mrs P had already been with her husband Ray for some time. The four of them became the best of friends and would spend holidays together, always having loads of fun. They spent many nights playing cards – Mrs P recalls the men always cheating, but not Mom; she would never cheat.

I've always known Mom was a purist, never speaking badly about anyone else, and Mrs P confirms that: 'Your mom never had a bad word to say about anybody, so different to me. I would love *koch* (harmless gossip) and she would stay silent – not all the time, but most of the time. She was a gentle soul and never intentionally hurt anyone. She had a heart of gold. She was an Eshet Chayil ['woman of valour', what Jewish people refer to as the perfect or ideal woman].'

When we emigrated to Australia in 1997, Mrs P said a part of her left too: 'I missed my bestest friend that

I'd ever had.' But they would speak often on the phone. Mrs P came to visit Mom in 2013, when she'd already been diagnosed with Alzheimer's. The two of them would get Freezochinos every day, spend hours lying in the sun and going for walks. Mrs P got to see Mom while she was still in good spirits and not yet completely overtaken by Alzheimer's, so she has the best of Mom as her memories. For me, so many of the good memories of Mom are eclipsed by the hard times, and they are much harder to live with.

Mom also got along famously with my aunt Ev, who was married to Dad's brother Mervyn. She said Mom was easygoing and full of fun: an innocent kind of naughty. 'We can't choose our family but we can choose our friends,' Ev would say, but she would have chosen Mom anyway. They would tell each other everything and they shared a really special bond. Ev would tell the story of how, one year, Mom and Dad met Ev and Mervyn in Queensland for a holiday. Ev loved to have a flutter on the slot machines, and Mom was always up for fun, so one night when all four were out walking, Ev and Mom slipped into a casino unbeknownst to Dad and Mervyn. Mervyn wasn't fazed – this was normal for Ev – but Dad was furious. Apparently after Mom had won a few times on the slot machines, she turned to Ev and said, 'They didn't want us to come in here and now we are winning.'

* * *

I was just shy of my thirteenth birthday when my family emigrated to Australia, and in some ways it felt like we'd swapped one life for another. Moving to Sydney's North Shore, my brothers and I went to a Jewish school with friends who had also emigrated from South Africa, so the adjustment was relatively easy. We found our places in sports teams and easily slotted into social groups. But it wasn't as easy for my parents. Dad had to build up a dental practice from scratch, and for many years he struggled with the transition. Mom bore the brunt of it and was the one who had to support Dad in these times. This went on for quite a few years, but Mom just took it in her stride. I think she carried the weight of the move from South Africa on her shoulders, but she felt it was her job to keep it together for the rest of us. Needless to say, during my childhood, Mom was always smiling – that was simply how she presented to the world.

Greg and Mom were close. When he talks about her, what he mostly remembers is how kind and caring she was, how she was us three kids' biggest ally and advocate. If Dad ever shouted at us, Mom would always go and speak to him on our behalf. She would call him out when she believed he was in the wrong. Greg describes her as being on the 'straight and narrow', and living quite a regimented life. She wasn't the overly adventurous type but she supported everything my brothers and I did and would schlep us everywhere.

Ricky, meanwhile, would tell all his friends that his mom was the best; he'd always be surprised when someone else thought *their* mother was the best. He has fond memories of Mom playing Lego with him for hours, building detailed houses, everything colour-coordinated. Ricky and Mom would also spend many Thursdays together, because my brother had a knack for being unwell on a Thursday and Mom would always let him stay home from school. Ricky also remembers Mom driving him everywhere, and how detailed her directions were. Back in the day, the only way to get around town was with a map book, and Mom would consult it intensively and meticulously write out directions – which was handy, as Ricky was playing soccer all over Sydney.

One thing about Mom was that she took great pride in her appearance. Perhaps that was why she became a beautician by profession, although the only time I can remember her working in the industry was back in Johannesburg, when she turned one of our spare rooms into a salon. Anyway, she always had her hair blow-dried and face made up. It was always subtle, never over the top – exactly like her personality. She never commanded attention, but she could light up a room with her presence.

One day she was driving out to Dad's dental practice, where she worked several days a week, and stopped at a traffic light to apply her lipstick. A police officer pulled up next to her, asked her to wind down her window, and proceeded to tell her she shouldn't be applying make-up while driving. But after experiencing her subtle charm and pure innocence, the police officer let her go without a ticket, just a smile.

* * *

Mom's mother, my *bobba* (Yiddish for 'grandmother'), remained in South Africa but would come and visit us in Sydney, as well as her other children and grandchildren who had also emigrated. Bobba and Mom were very close – they had the ultimate mother–daughter relationship. I think that Mom being the youngest of four kids and the only girl made that relationship easy. Mom and I didn't have that same mother–daughter bond, however, as I was closer to Dad. Deep down, I've always carried a sense of guilt about not being able to replicate the relationship Mom had with her own mother.

Bobba was visiting Sydney in 2003 for the birth of her first great-grandchild when she suffered a stroke and became paralysed from the neck down. This was a distressing time for the whole family. After Bobba had been in hospital for a few weeks, we were able to move her into a facility near our home, where I would visit her after school. The place very much had the feeling of a nursing home, or even a hospital, with Bobba in a small room.

Hindsight is always a wonderful thing. Over the years, I've often reflected on how traumatic this incident with Bobba would've been for Mom, but she never truly shared with any of us how she felt, or sought help for something of that personal magnitude. And I've found myself wondering how the associated stress of this might've fed into what was to happen to Mom with the Alzheimer's. It wasn't just the fact of the stroke. After three months in Australia, Bobba's travel insurance was going to stop covering her, so we needed to fly her back home. This eventually happened, but it wasn't a regular flight. Bobba and Mom had to be accompanied by a doctor and several nurses – a group that took up the back four rows of the plane – for the fourteen-hour flight to Johannesburg. I can only imagine how stressful this experience was. Then, once Bobba was settled into a nursing home, Mom would fly back to South Africa every few months to see her. On top of all this, Dad put pressure on her to not be away for long, because without her at home, he couldn't cope. When Bobba did pass away, Mom wasn't in South Africa, so she never had the opportunity to say goodbye. When she flew over for the funeral, Mom and her brothers had only a few days to pack up Bobba's apartment in Johannesburg.

I can now empathise with Mom, understanding the weight of losing a parent. Looking back, I don't think Mom ever really dealt with the trauma that surrounded her own mother's illness, or the circumstances that led to her passing. I do know that when Mom returned to Australia after the funeral, something in her had shifted. She now carried a sense of sadness and loss that never really went away.

Chapter 3

THE EARLY SIGNS

After Bobba's passing, Mom became more and more withdrawn, socialising with her friends less frequently, as if she had fallen into a depression. What we eventually came to learn was that Mom was very good at concealing what she was going through. When she struggled, which she certainly did in the period after her mother's death, she withdrew so as to not make it our problem. This pattern continued over a number of years, with changes so subtle they were barely noticeable in everyday life, but which were compounding internally.

When we'd come to Sydney from South Africa, Mom had taken control of everything: organising us kids at a new school, preparing the house, taking care of Dad, settling us all into our new life. But now, simple tasks that had been second nature became more complex for her. She started forgetting things, or completely freaking out at not being able to do something simple. It was confusing for the whole family, especially as it seemed to have come out of nowhere and made no sense, which unfortunately resulted in my father, brothers and me becoming increasingly frustrated with Mom.

It was 2010 and we were getting ready to travel to Israel for a cousin's wedding, and Mom needed to buy a dress. I met her at Chatswood Chase, a shopping centre we'd frequented for years, and after she'd picked out and bought a dress, we walked together to the car park, to which we'd both driven separately. Mom became very agitated and stressed; I saw a look of fear come over her, but I couldn't understand why. It turned out she could not for the life of her remember where she'd parked her car, and she started crying. I had never seen this behaviour from Mom before, and it concerned me. How could she not remember where she'd parked when we'd been going to that place for so long? I tried to remain calm but couldn't, and ended up raising my voice out of frustration and disbelief. I suggested we retrace her steps, but she could not comprehend what I was saying, and this only made her more stressed. She was so unsure and confused. We literally walked up and down the car park until we finally found her vehicle.

At home, I brushed off what had happened, chalking it up to an off day. I certainly didn't think I'd just seen signs of Alzheimer's.

The first week of the Israel trip was incredible, with our whole extended family having come together. We all started off in Tel Aviv, then my parents, uncles, aunts and grandparents went off touring up north together, while my cousin, brothers and I made our own way, meeting the others along the way in different locations. It was easy, uncomplicated fun. The wedding in Jerusalem was also a hit, and Mom seemed to be having a great time, smiling and dancing. Then, one night, we were in our apartment, getting ready to go out, and Mom was looking for a particular skirt she wanted to wear. When she couldn't find it, she became distressed and extremely irrational. Eventually I found the skirt and she calmed down, but it was as if, the moment she realised she couldn't find the skirt, she'd lost control. It was somewhat reminiscent of a toddler who hasn't fully developed the ability to control their emotions, and it's impossible to rationalise with them. No amount of talking or reassurance would have calmed Mom down. It was an echo of the car park incident, but not significant enough on its own to trigger any alarm bells.

Later that year I had ankle surgery. Under normal circumstances, Mom would have been the first one to volunteer to take me to the hospital. But she refused to drive me there, which I found very strange. In retrospect, I now believe she was self-aware enough at the time to know she wasn't comfortable with driving a long distance to somewhere unfamiliar, but at the time she didn't express that to me. I was infuriated about having to catch a taxi – my father and brothers couldn't take me because of work commitments – and genuinely baffled by the situation.

On another occasion, Greg found himself helping Mom prepare a Business Activity Statement (BAS) for the tax office. It was strange, because while accounting and numbers were not her forte, she had been doing the BAS ever since we'd moved to Australia and was generally competent at putting it together. But now she was making lots of mistakes. Dad would get angry at her for messing it up, then Greg would try to help her rectify the mess and he too would get frustrated. None of us read too much into it, but Mom was having real difficulties with repetitive tasks that had once been so simple.

Greg had moved to Sydney's eastern suburbs after university and I'd followed him once I finished studying. My parents and Ricky eventually decided to make the move, too, so we would all live within a few kilometres of one another. While they were preparing to do so, Greg's wife Lee-Anne had a conversation with Mom about packing up the house. Lee suggested that Mom get rid of the stuff she no longer needed or wanted, as my parents were downsizing. Mom could only look at Lee with pure confusion and say, 'But I don't know how to do that.'

I'll give one more example. Mom worked at Dad's dental practice for years, where she was well known and loved by all – so much so that we often joked she wasn't there to work but rather to chat to all the staff and patients. She was extremely competent, handling patient appointments, taking payments and doing general admin. Suddenly, she couldn't remember how to perform these previously familiar, simple tasks. I can only imagine how frustrating this would have been for her, knowing something wasn't right but unable to pinpoint what was going on.

* * *

Those early signs were small but significant. And countless moments like these were to follow, where the rest of the family would become frustrated with Mom because we had no idea why she was suddenly acting like this, as if she had lost all her confidence.

I still can't comprehend how it all happened. Was it due to her lifestyle, her genes, or just bad luck? How can someone so young, so vibrant and capable, suddenly lose their ability to perform tasks they'd done so effortlessly for so long? We have all experienced a moment where we've forgotten something or misplaced an item, an instant that feels like a temporary loss of memory. Typically those moments are fleeting. But imagine forgetting something, and then forgetting something else, and it only getting worse. Imagine suddenly losing your ability to do what had always been so easy, and not being able to understand why. The only small bit of comfort I can take from that whole period is that when she was losing her memory, my mom for the most part was likely unaware of what was happening – at least, I hope that was the case.

Over the first two years of these changes, because Mom was only in her fifties and dementia was simply not on our radar, there was simply no motivation to look into it. For one thing, my family had no history of Alzheimer's, and none of us thought it was prevalent among adults in their forties or fifties. Maybe we were in denial, but we just could not comprehend why Mom was acting this way: withdrawn, forgetful, depressed. It seemed inexplicable. Only when we had a diagnosis did things start to fall into place.

In the wake of what happened to my mother, Professor Henry Brodaty, an expert on dementia and ageing from the University of New South Wales, and who I was introduced to through my work with the Centre for Healthy Brain Ageing or CHeBA (which I describe in Chapter 8), has helped me to better comprehend what my family was dealing with. Here's a summary of some of what I've learned from him.

Dementia is the umbrella term for a group of cognitive diseases, of which Alzheimer's is the most common. Dementia presents as a decline in one or more cognitive areas, including memory, language and executive abilities (planning, organisation, abstract thinking or conceptual shifting, and visual–spatial processing), and this decline impairs day-to-day functioning that may be personal, such as managing finances, driving, or organisational or occupational tasks. Early signs include difficulty in learning new material, forgetting things, problems following stories, and difficulty finding words or getting organised. Symptoms typical of Alzheimer's are short-term memory loss, as evidenced by forgetting conversations or repeating questions; word-finding difficulties; impaired judgement; and personality changes. Other signs might be apathy (for example, losing interest in hobbies), anxiety or depression, or impaired instrumental functions. Early-onset dementia, which is also called young-onset dementia, is when the disease begins in people younger than sixty-five years of age.

Professor Brodaty explained to me that when you ask most people what they have trouble remembering, they most often say 'names', and so he doesn't believe this is a reliable marker for early dementia. But if people start forgetting conversations or appointments or continually repeating themselves, those are concerning signs that are worth investigating. Brodaty said that more weight should be given to what other people notice as unusual behaviour for an individual. For example, if a person doesn't typically have a good sense of direction, then there would be little cause for concern if they find it difficult to navigate.

It is also important to understand that different types of dementia have different symptoms. For example, Lewy body dementia causes movement disorders during sleep, whereas in frontotemporal dementia, a person's memory is preserved for longer but their behaviour becomes strange and often results in psychiatric consultations.

According to Brodaty, if you have a family history of dementia, it does increase your own risk of developing the disease. There are also subtypes of Alzheimer's. About 1 per cent of Alzheimer's cases are autosomal-dominant, meaning they are due to a genetic disorder caused by mutations of the amyloid precursor protein (APP) or presenilin (PSEN) genes – if you have such a gene, it is certain that you will get the disease, usually in your forties or fifties. There is a gene test available but it is not the whole picture. Personally, I have no desire to get tested and then live with the knowledge either way. I'd rather adopt a healthy lifestyle. For most people, however, dementia is a late-onset disease, with the risk doubling every five years for the elderly. In addition, we know that 40 per cent of the risk of dementia is due to environmental factors that we can do something about. I talk about this in detail later in the book.

* * *

When everything started to unravel, Ricky, who was studying law at university, was still living at home with Mom and Dad; Greg and I had already moved out. This meant that Ricky was the one in the trenches. I can honestly say I never realised, nor appreciated, the position he was in, what it was like for him, until, after Mom had passed away, he shared with me some thoughts he'd written down. While I can't change the past, I am so grateful for this, and for the deeper understanding I now have of how difficult it was at home. Ricky has a whole journal of notes that he wrote at the time, mostly from when he was still living at home with my parents in the early days. I didn't know about this journal until I told him about the book and he then shared it with me. It was harrowing to read. Here is an excerpt from Ricky's journal:

It started a few years ago, I can't really recall the date. My initial memory leads me to Mom's uncertainty and ultimately inability to provide Dad with directions from home to a place in Gordon, just near the train station ... [M]any years before, Mom was so confident and skilled at reading maps and providing directions. This distance was only a few kms and an area she knew so well, yet she couldn't do it. She asked me to help – she couldn't grasp which way we would be driving on the map and constantly got her left and right confused ... she seemed unsure and was waiting for me to give guidance before giving an answer.

This behaviour continued in a variety of facets ... since immigration Mom has been running the accounts for my dad's dental practice. Granted, she was never amazing at completing these tasks, but she was more than capable ... again, over the last few years she has become unconfident with completing these tasks – specifically getting the date incorrect as it is based on the American system. Now, I would think that after doing this for so long, it would become simple, perhaps muscle memory would take over and guide her ... but no, this is not what happened, and to this day she still is unsure and gets these tasks incorrect ...

I'll be honest – and I hate myself for writing, thinking, saying this – but there was a point where I questioned if my mom was stupid. Because I ... [got] to see example after example, I wondered and questioned her intellect. I again hate myself for the way I reacted then, but I constantly lost my temper and shouted ... 'How can you not get this, we have been over this time and time again, it is so simple' –

and then I would watch my mom cry and she would tell
herself that she is so stupid ... I feel so stupid! At times,
I just looked at her and often felt annoyed for the position
she put me in – like it was her fault that she wasn't getting it.

Time and time again this happened – I would explain
tasks, she wouldn't get it [and] I would lose my temper, and
as much as I tried to control myself, I often let it slip and
then the whole process of crying and shame would start all
over again. Often I would have to leave as these tasks which
should only take a few minutes to explain and understand
were just before I had to go somewhere – and I wonder
how she felt when I left. I thought about it then, and now ...
I remember calling Greg and ... telling him how bad I felt.

No-one witnessed the deterioration of Mom more than
Ricky and Dad. They bore the brunt of it all. Greg and I
had a buffer – our own homes to go to – and we escaped
the harsh daily reality. It was evident to me that Ricky
was not coping well, but I never truly understood the
gravitas of the situation, and how living at home put him
in a position of responsibility Greg and I weren't privy to.
When Ricky left the house for work each morning, he was
riddled with guilt for leaving, especially on the days when
Mom didn't have much planned. On those days, Mom
would call Ricky multiple times throughout the day for no
apparent reason. When his phone rang, he always had the

sickening feeling that something bad had happened, but mostly Mom was filling in time and asking him arbitrary questions, like whether he wanted her to iron his pants or what he wanted for dinner. Dad, meanwhile, often tried to use humour with Mom to make light of the situation, but she didn't respond well to this; it only made her more sensitive to what was happening. At other times, Dad would show anger, as Ricky explained in his journal:

I can hear Mom crying and calling me ... She is crying and visibly upset – more than upset, this is a state I have never seen before. Dad shouted at her and she has lost all control of her emotions. I lost it at him but controlled myself and marched them into the TV room and told Dad he cannot do that! His actions are completely unacceptable, but I realised the stress my dad has been under, and I understand his frustration got the better of him. To be honest he had been handling the whole thing very well given the circumstances and had been the rock holding Mom and I together since the move to the east [of Sydney].

I also told Mom that there is simply no choice – she has got to go see a doctor as we are all worried for her and the situation. I left them to sort it out ... When I look back now, I think my actions were a part of the reason we took this to the level we did. Of course, it was all of us – but this episode made us realise right in front of our eyes that something is just not right, that something could be seriously wrong.

I knew that things at my parents' home were hard, as I communicated with my brothers and father all the time. But no words could convey what everyone was going through. Things with Mom in the early years went up and down – we would have good days and some really bad days. She could go from normal and happy to crying and upset in a matter of moments. But we didn't know what we were dealing with, so we weren't equipped to take care of Mom. This was a note Ricky wrote recording his feelings at that time:

It's been a month since I last wrote and things have been OK with Mom. She has been openly asking me how to do things and I've been helping ... and been very calm. Today, however, I have come home after gym and Mom is crying. She tells me Dad said something which upset her, something about being useless, but she wasn't sure. So I wanted to get Dad's side before anything was done.

Yes, Dad can be too short, but this is all new for all of us and no-one knows how to deal with it since we don't know the prognosis. I don't think Dad's dealing with it too well, but it is so hard – he works so hard in a stressful environment and after a ten-hour day he can obviously be tired, and

things don't come across the way I assume he intends.
I think tomorrow we should talk, and I should tell him that
no-one is against him but we all need to be more sensitive to
Mom because I believe she is not in a good place right now.

* * *

Those early days tested us all. We all had moments, many moments, when we lost it due to pure frustration and confusion about what was happening. I can only reflect on the situation here in this book, in the hope that the next person who encounters what we did will be better equipped to deal with it.

Would my family have done anything differently had we been better educated about dementia? I'd like to think so, if it had been under our control. But the resources simply weren't there and we had knowledge gaps. We were in the thick of it without guidance, trying to survive, trying to care for Mom, trying to care for each other. And even at that point, we still didn't know what we were dealing with.

Chapter 4

THE DIAGNOSIS

Mom was in good health for most of her life. I couldn't recall a time when she was ever sick other than with a cold or another equally common ailment. She never complained about feeling poorly, never exhibited any real signs of illness or disease or injury, so it was hard to imagine Mom unwell – I didn't know what that looked like. Up until the events of June 2011, I lived with the belief that my parents would only get sick when they were very old, or they would simply die of old age. When Mom started presenting with unusual behaviour, it wasn't as though we completely ignored it, or were in denial about it, but it simply didn't compute that this could be serious or that anything bad could happen to her. Dad genuinely thought that, if anything, he would die before Mom, so much so that he only bothered getting life insurance for himself. If anything ever happened to him, he figured, she would be covered. But that's life, full of unwanted surprises.

Mom had been working at Dad's dental practice since he opened it in 1998. As I mentioned earlier, she knew the place inside and out, and all the staff and patients loved her presence, her calm and friendly nature. She socialised more than she worked, but Dad didn't mind – I think he was only too happy to just have Mom there during the day. Patients could feel her kindness when they interacted with her, and she was always present when she was speaking with them; a true asset to any business. However, the issues with the Business Activity Statement (BAS) kept occurring and began to impact the business.

Dad's accountant had called him to ask what was wrong with Mom. When Dad said he wasn't aware what the accountant was referring to, the man proceeded to say that the BAS was 'a dog's breakfast'. This was in some ways the catalyst for my family seeking help, the beginning of what led to the diagnosis. There had been many incidents by now, and taken together, something clearly wasn't right and we couldn't ignore it anymore. Dad took my mom to a GP near his dental practice and thus began the process of investigating what we were dealing with.

Dad first talked to the GP by himself, rather than discuss what had been happening in front of Mom – she always hated people talking about her and not *to* her. Then Dad took Mom to the GP, who had her perform the Mini-Mental State Examination (MMSE), which is a screening text for cognitive impairment. Mom became uneasy and then distraught during the test because she couldn't remember the sequence of answers she was required to memorise. The doctor then suggested that Mom see a neurologist.

The anticipation around that first doctor's appointment was intense, because ignorance is bliss. I remember anxiously awaiting the outcome at home. Earlier, Ricky had written about his own fears:

> I just worry for Mom. We all need to be there for her – that may mean putting our lives on hold for the sake and benefit of her. I don't believe this is true ... but I wonder if Ke [Keri] and Greg ever forget what is going on with Mom on a day-to-day basis because they don't see everything I see whilst I am living at home.

As it turned out, that appointment was only the beginning. We didn't get any answers that day, just the start of a deeper investigation.

Mom was referred to a neurologist at St Vincent's Hospital, who first did a series of brain scans to rule out a tumour. There was no evidence of one, so we were now closing in on a diagnosis. There was some relief at this news, but also some frustration, as we wanted an answer to what was going on. The neurologist suggested Mom needed to have a positron emission tomography (PET) scan, which is an imaging test that uses radioactive material to diagnose brain disorders, heart disease and other conditions. This was apparently the only way to determine if we were in fact dealing with dementia, which now seemed the likeliest scenario. As luck would have it, a colleague of the neurologist was doing a research project on diagnosing dementia and he arranged for Mom to go have the scan in Melbourne – although she wouldn't be part of the research.

At this point, we still had not received a final diagnosis, but even so, what we were dealing with was becoming clearer. And yet the possibility of Alzheimer's was confusing. How could that be? Wasn't Mom too young? Don't only old people get Alzheimer's? Besides, no-one in our family had a history of Alzheimer's. What was going on?

Greg flew to Melbourne with Mom. It couldn't have been easy as Mom was aware something was wrong, but Greg was calm and had all the patience in the world. It helped that, according to Greg, Mom wasn't overly anxious or worried, but rather generally level-headed that day. One could only suspect she was nervous about what was coming, but I think she only had a vague understanding of what was going on: she knew something was wrong but couldn't really comprehend it all, so didn't show any outward signs of great concern. In the end, it was a quick trip: after the doctor explained the process, Mom had the scan, which took thirty minutes, and then she and Greg were on their way back to the airport.

That was 17 June 2011. On 20 June, we received the following report from the Department of Nuclear Medicine at the Royal Melbourne Hospital:

Clinical History

54-year-old female with suspected early-onset Alzheimer's disease.

Procedure

A 30-minute PET acquisition was performed 40 minutes after injection of 376 MBq C1 1 PUB.

Report

There is extensive cortisol binding of BIP, particularly in the frontal, lateral temporal and posterior cingulate/ precuneus cortex. There is also binding in the caudate nuclei. There is relative sparing of occipital and primary sensorimotor cortex.

Conclusion

The PIB scan shows extensive cortical amyloid plaque
consistent with Alzheimer's disease.

Mom had just been officially diagnosed with early-onset
Alzheimer's. She was just three weeks shy of her fifty-fifth
birthday.

I don't remember exactly where I was when we got the
diagnosis. I assume I would have gone over to Dad's place
and he would have explained the results to me. What I do
know is that, even though Alzheimer's had been raised as a
possibility in the months leading up to the diagnosis, there
was a part of me that had clung to the hope that this was
all a bad dream. So having it confirmed was shocking, gut-
wrenching. I think I've erased a lot about that day from
my memory. I know I came home and cried. I also know I
told hardly any of my friends. I was still confused but also
ashamed, and part of me was in denial, so it was easier
not to talk about it. My family was officially entering
uncharted waters and it was scary.

Still, news can travel quickly in our community. An old
schoolfriend, someone I hadn't spoken to in a while, texted
me to say she was sorry about the news and was there for
me. I was livid. I remember calling Greg and yelling about
it – how dare she message me! I wasn't really angry at her,
though, but rather I was angry about the diagnosis, about

the fact that Mom was going to be different and I didn't know what it all meant.

After the diagnosis, my siblings, Dad and I experienced different things at different times: sometimes we felt a sense of relief because we now knew what was going on, and we could better help Mom; and sometimes we felt anger and shame. But sometimes none of us knew how to feel. Ricky, who was in Israel for a one-month internship when he got the news, summed up the confusion of feelings in his journal:

Just sat down for lunch at a café in Ramat Gan and I answer a call from my dad. I had forgotten when we were getting the results of the scan, but ... for some reason I knew what it was about when he said hi. It's weird, the results are exactly what I expected but at the same time exactly what I didn't expect. Although I believed it couldn't be anything but Alzheimer's, at the same time I didn't really believe it would be. I never wanted this to be the result but also, I felt if it wasn't this – then what was it?

This was the first time in my life ... that I can recall where speaking to my dad, he broke down ... I teared up and so did he. I am uncertain of the scientific circumstances surrounding the diagnosis, but I have been told this degenerative disease ... can be quick. 1–2 years and she won't be able to drive, 5–10 could be or quite likely will be her life expectancy.

We had no idea then about how accurate the diagnosis was. It was a lot to take in and process, and we always held some hope that the doctors got it wrong. But life changed pretty quickly. Everything was unknown, something new we needed to navigate, and there was no rule book. The first thing we learned was that we were now living in Mom's world, and it was us who needed to adapt to the situation and her new normal.

And yet, despite the trauma relating to the diagnosis and everything that happened in the weeks, months and years that followed, it wasn't all doom and gloom. Ricky again:

It has been a strange week or so since we found out the diagnosis ... Mom is what she was like a few years ago. It is so strange! The phone conversations have been amazing: she is vibrant, talkative, aware, and [it] honestly feels like she is what she once was. I spoke to her yesterday and she was filling me in on her entire weekend, including who they [her and Dad] saw, where they ate on Saturday night, where they were about to go ... I got this sliver of hope that maybe she is OK. But I realise it is probably not the case ... [Still] I expect I will remember that conversation.

From what Greg and Ke have told me thus far ... since she has been diagnosed it is like a weight is off her shoulders. She has no more tests to 'look forward to', as that was her biggest worry. I don't think it was the results but the fact of being tested … she hated it because I think she felt like she was made to feel stupid, which she obviously isn't. [And] since she has been diagnosed, she has been so positive. It is amazing and so unexpected. When I think about it, that is my mom. She is always the positive one …

Maybe this wasn't a strange week but a good week and hopefully we will have plenty more of them. I am very grateful though for the people around my mom, including obviously Greg and Ke, Lee and Lauren [Ricky's partner] and of course Dad who it seems before was on a mission to ensure people did not forget about my mom. He was so forceful in a positive way to make sure people took her out – and now I hope that will continue. I will be forever grateful to those people – but time is a funny thing and we will see how long people remember for.

* * *

Our family was strong. We got on well, shared lots of silly jokes and laughs between us. Before Mom's diagnosis, we'd never really dealt with any great hardship. We'd been lucky. Greg had thyroid cancer in his early twenties but it wasn't life-threatening – he underwent an operation to remove his thyroid and made a full recovery. Don't get me wrong, that was a scary time for us: cancer in your early twenties is a tough pill to swallow. But Mom's dementia felt much bigger. Never in my wildest imaginings had I thought that something like this could impact us as a family unit.

After the initial shock of the diagnosis, Dad went into survival mode: he focused 100 per cent on Mom, a sort of tunnel vision that meant he couldn't see things from any other perspective. But this was new to all of us, and we needed a game plan for how to cope. Most importantly, we needed to know what we had to do for Mom, and what the next few years would look like. We couldn't do this alone; we needed help from professionals.

I remember the first time we went to the home of a dementia specialist and sat together as a family to talk about Alzheimer's and what was going to happen to Mom. A picture was painted of what the next few years might look like, the stages in which things could happen: Mom losing her memory, forgetting who we were, losing her ability to speak, to walk, to perform bodily functions. We were told that she'd get to the point where she would have no real ability to function whatsoever, when even swallowing would become impossible, and she would eventually pass away. We were told we would all need to see a therapist, and that this whole experience would rock our family in unimaginable ways.

The dementia specialist referred to Alzheimer's as a 'death sentence'. At the time, those words seemed very

# The Long Goodbye

harsh, but they would prove an accurate representation. A person with Alzheimer's is trapped: they have no control over their declining brain function nor anything else that is happening to them. Ricky captured what we all felt:

That first meeting was an eye-opener. That is when I broke down, but I thought to myself, *Fuck It! I am upset, I am allowed to cry, so don't feel ashamed, this is a sad time.* From the moment she [the specialist] started speaking, with 'I will explain 30 per cent of what I know and you will probably only remember 10 per cent' ... she was so honest and did not sugar-coat anything, that I really respected her. Mostly what I got out of tonight was the point of asking my mom what she wants. We have been speaking about all these ideas and procedures we may implement to help my mom, but firstly we must ask what she wants ... It was basically explained that this is a serious disease, not to her [Mom's] intelligence and feelings, but to her memory. Obviously there will be other damaging effects, but she is not stupid and is well aware of what is going on. Thus, don't treat her like a baby, but more importantly there are ways to approach certain things. Ask her how her day was, not what she did. If you know she spent time with Aaron [her first grandchild], ask her how her day with Aaron was ...

She may get angry and aggressive, she may forget our names, she may ask the same question over and over again, she may get worse in the late afternoon [the 'sundown' effect] but she will never forget that she loves us! I like that … I guess for me the saddest day will be when it is either so confronting or maybe when she loses her ability to be resourceful and that is the day she loses her independence and maybe a part of her dies. Maybe I get my independence from her, something I never knew where I got it from?

As Ricky noted, our sessions with the dementia specialist were important for learning how to speak to Mom. The most important thing was to never test her. We had to ask questions she could answer simply – direct questions that would prompt a straight answer. We had to avoid asking questions which would require her to think and construct a response.

Beyond professional help, there were people who, no matter what was going on in their own lives, made time for Mom and looked after us. Mom had an amazing friend, Lynn, who gave her time so selflessly. Lynn would take Mom walking almost every week while Mom was still able to. It was so important for her to get out with friends and maintain some independence. It was also important for her to feel as though she was still contributing to the family, which is why Dad suggested to Lynn that they could walk to the bank to draw the wages for Dad's staff. Mom was thrilled about this; she felt empowered that she could do that. Lynn would stand at the door of the bank and let Mom go in and make the transactions, never intervening until such time as Mom simply wasn't able to do it herself anymore. Lynn helped Mom maintain her sense of self-worth and never made her feel inadequate.

The dementia specialist had told us it was vital for Mom to be set up with a psychologist. That person ultimately came to work with Mom at home for a period of almost three years, up until she moved into a nursing home. Those sessions were helpful for Mom, although we knew she didn't always love them or want to be there. I think they allowed her to work through what she was feeling, to validate what was happening to her and to have someone advocating for her. After only a couple of sessions, Mom was more up-front with us about how she was feeling and what she was going through. She expressed that she was having difficulty in maintaining an understanding of conversations when there was a lot of content or a lot of people speaking; for instance, there were times when she would go out with a group of friends but couldn't follow the conversation and so withdrew. We had to be coached on how to deal with all of this. It wasn't second nature – it was new to all of us.

After one particular session with the psychologist, Mom seemed angry. She felt most comfortable talking to Ricky than anyone else, and she confided to him that she thought people were talking about her behind her back – not necessarily in a bad way, more being uncertain about how to approach her. It was actually good to see Mom showing some emotion. And she was right, people were talking about her. Friends were unsure of how to treat her, how to engage with her at the shops or in a social environment, and she was very aware of it.

* * *

Some of what Ricky wrote in his journal during his time at home with Mom was initially very hard to read, like getting a dagger to the heart. He had a special insight into Mom's new reality, and it was confronting to learn the ways in which the rest of us initially fell short during that steep learning curve.

Tonight I saw my mom trying desperately to reach out to my sister, asking her if she needs help to pack, asking her if she wants to take food home so she doesn't need to buy [any], but my sister failed to take the bait. All my mom wants is to be close to her and for her not to struggle. She mentioned many times in the conversation how worried she is for Ke and how Greg and I must try and get her to open up. Of course we will, but I just hope Ke and Mom break their barriers and open up to each other.

The Long Goodbye

There has always been a part of me that has been riddled with guilt for not giving Mom the mother–daughter relationship she longed for. As I said earlier in this book, it's just not who I am. I love differently. I've always felt strong enough to navigate my feelings alone and not let them affect anyone else, and I've always struggled with the old-school mentality of what is expected of a woman. After Mom was diagnosed, Dad had this expectation that, as I was the daughter, I'd take over the cooking and fill Mom's shoes. I strongly challenged those expectations and the associated idea of a woman's place in the world. Ironically, though, in a lot of ways I am like Mom. She was quite closed herself, always just getting on with things and never bothering anyone else with her feelings. When she did start to talk to a therapist and open up to Ricky, it was a window into a part of Mom we hadn't seen before.

My dad mentioned the other day how he wished my mom had always been this positive and open. This disease is so horrible, yet it has strangely opened my mom up. She is a different person and is reminiscent of the mom I thought I remembered. A while ago Greg and I spoke [about] how we couldn't really remember what my mom was like a while ago when she was what we considered normal – where she did things, met people, took the initiative ... strangely, how she is now is how I think she was before – obviously different but similar in certain respects.

Ricky reminded me of a time when Mom called me to tell me how she was feeling. It was amazing seeing her take control of this. It was as if, in some weird way, she had become more in tune with her emotions and expressiveness. That's the funny but also horrific thing about Alzheimer's: in certain moments, it felt as though Mom was making significant progress as a person. However, these moments wouldn't last long, and they would soon be overshadowed by another dip, introducing us to a new stage of the disease.

Many things upset Mom during those first few years. She became very emotional, which she may have always been but had hidden, or maybe all the emotions were new to her and she needed an outlet. In any case, she became unpredictable. Something would happen that ordinarily would be of no consequence, but now Mom was sensitive. She would go from happy to sad in a split second. She would be talking about something calmly and then drift off into another world, suddenly reappearing all angry and upset. One evening at home, someone broke a glass, and while Dad was cleaning it up he told Mom not to walk into the kitchen as she didn't have shoes on. Mom flew into a rage, so angry with Dad for telling her not to enter the kitchen. Once so stable, Mom's mood could now change without any warning; she was put on antidepressants to control this, which did settle her a bit.

Mom was doing it tough. Her world had changed dramatically. She spent most days mooching around the house, or walking to the shops and back. We tried many different activities to keep Mom active and engaged, such as dusting off our old tennis racquets. Mom had been a keen tennis player back in the day; in fact, our whole family grew up playing tennis. I loved those tennis games. It wasn't about winning, which it usually is for me, but rather being out together, doing something that Mom was capable of doing and could enjoy with us.

Mom also knew how to knit, so we suggested she start doing this again. For several years, she knitted scarves for us and blankets for the babies. She was so proud of what she had created, and so were we. When she told us she was having trouble casting off, we brought in someone who could help her do it when needed. Dad would sometimes take Mom to work with him, where she would sit out the back knitting. She could knit for hours – I think she had lost all sense of time by this point. One day, Dad came to check on her between patients, and seemingly out of nowhere there was an outburst of tears. Apparently she had been trying to cast off the needle for three hours but just couldn't remember how.

When Dad shared these stories with the rest of the family, we would naturally tear up. To hear about what was happening to Mom, and to see Dad's reaction, was too much to handle. I often asked myself, *How is it that someone can be robbed of so many things in such a short space of time?* Dementia really is a cruel and unforgiving disease.

The most obvious signs of deterioration arose in the home, small but significant. Mom would try to instruct you on how to do something that had once been second nature to her, and she would get confused, especially with sequencing: doing things in a particular order. One time she was trying to explain to Ricky how to defrost something, and instead of saying, 'Put it in the microwave for three minutes,' she said, 'Push one, one, one.' Another time, instead of saying, 'Put the towel in the laundry,' she handed me a towel and said, 'Put it in that room.'

Mom's Alzheimer's significantly impacted all of us, but she was particularly harsh on Dad. He took the brunt of everything. Unfortunately, we were all so concerned with Mom and the situation in general that we didn't really think too much about taking care of ourselves, or each other. Dad had an immense amount of pressure on him to keep everything together and care for Mom, but it's important for the caregiver to have a break. The thing is, Dad didn't really have an outlet or hobby where he could go and disconnect. He probably wouldn't have allowed himself to anyway. Mom and Dad had done everything together since they were married. Dad didn't know life without Mom.

There were many times in those first few years when someone exploded. Tension was high, our emotions were all over the place, and we didn't have a blueprint for managing what we were experiencing. Often, we each had an opinion on how things should be done. There were many arguments, many times when we erupted out of pure frustration and miscommunication. We had countless family meetings to mediate for each other and resolve the arguments we found ourselves having.

In amongst the trials and tribulations, though, the real victim was always Mom. She couldn't control what was happening to her, and in turn to all of us.

* * *

In an effort to better care for Mom, and also track her condition as she continued to decline, Dad contacted a professor at St Vincent's Hospital who was the head of dementia research, asking him if he could manage Mom's case. The professor agreed to see Mom every month, in order to monitor her condition and prescribe medical care as necessary. Mom was petrified about attending these appointments; she couldn't understand why she had to go into such a clinical environment, and she would inevitably cry, not wanting to be there. My dad and the doctors did explain what was happening, but she could not comprehend the detail. She was also scared because she knew she would 'fail' the tests and that would upset her. Intuitively, she knew she was sick. Nonetheless, the professor would perform the necessary neurological tests on Mom to determine where she was at in the Alzheimer's cycle.

After a year of such tests, the professor told Dad that he was very concerned about Mom's condition, with her most recent examination being particularly discouraging. She had been put on medication in the hope of slowing the progress of the disease, but the drugs were simply not working as well as hoped. This was awful news – we had never been given false hope that we could beat the disease, but neither had we realised how quickly Mom would deteriorate. We felt that time was against us.

It was after we'd entered the second year post-diagnosis that the professor told us that, in the next six to twelve months, it was likely Mom would wake up and not know who we were.

Chapter 5

THE FIRST FEW YEARS

With Mom's diagnosis came a sense of relief at being able to put a label on what was happening to her, although that label held a lot of uncertainty for what lay ahead. We may have finally known what was troubling Mom, but it opened us up to more complications than we could ever have anticipated. For one thing, Alzheimer's is a strange disease in that a person who has it can be acutely aware of what they are not comfortable with.

One of my earlier memories following Mom's diagnosis was when Mom stopped driving outside of the area where she lived. She had been driving all over Sydney ever since we'd moved there, but suddenly she refused to take the car out to Dad's practice, or back to the North Shore where she had stayed for many years. She realised she wasn't comfortable doing this anymore, so she made sure she didn't have to.

Being an avid cook and baker, Mom had always been able to whip up all sorts of things without following a recipe. Now, however, she was clearly more comfortable relying on instructions in a cookbook. She never verbalised this to us, but we noticed her using recipes, which was something she didn't ordinarily do.

It was amazing to see how, even in these circumstances, Mom would become resourceful. When she needed something from the shops, instead of driving, she would walk, intent on maintaining her independence. We knew it was important for us to encourage this, so whenever we needed something from the shops, we would ask her if she would go and get it. This helped Mom continue to be involved in our daily lives, rather than being made to feel redundant. Never underestimate a person; empower them instead. And so Dad would write down lists of things Mom could buy for us, to help her feel important and useful.

Still, I can only imagine how much time Mom spent at home feeling lonely and depressed. At the time, Mom and Dad lived in a ground-floor apartment, but because of how the building was situated, there wasn't a great deal of natural light and it could get very dark inside. This is not good for people with Alzheimer's, as they can experience 'sundowning', which is when an absence of sunlight alters one's disposition and prompts strong mood swings. It also causes sleeping problems, which can manifest in confusion, anxiety, agitation, pacing or disorientation that begins at dusk and continues throughout the night.

Professor Henry Brodaty explained to me that late afternoon is always the worst time for dementia sufferers, who can get irritable and tired then. The reasons for this are not entirely known, but it could be a kind of fatiguing that occurs towards the end of the day, especially when the sun goes down. Brodaty advises the families of people with Alzheimer's to try getting the person to have a nap after lunch, while ensuring this does not extend beyond forty-five minutes – this will prevent them from going into REM sleep, which could interfere with their night-time sleep. He also said it is important for dementia sufferers to be exposed to sunlight. Sunlight can help calibrate the diurnal rhythm of the circadian clock inside the brain, as sunlight stimulates the pituitary gland to produce melatonin. Brodaty added that around 90 per cent of people in nursing homes are deficient in vitamin D, which makes them more likely to suffer fractures. More evidence is emerging that sunlight is essential to human health, but especially to those who are affected by Alzheimer's. It could be the difference between a good day and a bad day.

Dad pleaded with the building's strata committee to allow him to change the windows in the apartment to alleviate my mom's Alzheimer's-associated depression. However, the request was denied on the basis that it would interfere with the aesthetics of the building, even though the windows could not be seen from street level. It was infuriating how a faceless committee could prioritise the minor aesthetics of a building over someone's health. The people involved had no idea how something so simple could have such a profound impact on my mom.

I do wish people showed more empathy and consideration for those living with life-altering conditions, whether it be a disease or a disability. Perhaps it's because of my life experiences, or maybe it's innate, but if I can make someone's life easier, I will do so without hesitation. Sometimes, rules and policies are out of date or simply out of touch with reality, and there are times when you must put the welfare of others ahead of by-laws. Throughout my mother's journey, I saw the best and worst of people.

* * *

As previously mentioned, Mom would walk down to the shops most days, if not several times a day. The local café owners and shop employees knew her – she had that effect on people, being so warm and friendly. They were also prepared for Mom's visits, as Dad had alerted them to the situation so they could help if Mom was confused or unsure of where she was. One of her daily buys was a Freezochino, which is a creamy iced coffee. In fact, whenever you saw Mom, she would have a Freezochino in hand. She would buy one in the morning and sip it throughout the day. Sometimes she would buy one, forget that she had done so, and then go and buy another one. Suddenly there were all these Freezochinos in the freezer.

I hated those things. Sure, they taste good, but they are full of sugar, and it pained me that Mom would drink one or two of them every day. I really wanted to stop her from having them, partly because I was becoming aware of the connection between Alzheimer's and diet and general lifestyle. But then again, that daily drink provided Mom with so much joy, and I wasn't going to take one of life's few remaining pleasures away from her.

As time wore on, buying Freezochinos and other goods was no longer as straightforward as it used to be. Simple things, such as using cash to pay for groceries, had become complex tasks for Mom. She would open her purse and become completely confused or unable to count out the necessary money. If I was with her, I'd usually take her purse and make the payment for her – I know I should have let her try to do it herself, but often there would be a line of people behind us, waiting to pay, and I would get a little frustrated.

It was worse when there was a 'first': the first time she misplaced her keys, the first time she said she didn't want to drive, the first time she couldn't do an easy admin task. I would instinctively belittle Mom because I was in disbelief that she couldn't do simple tasks that she had previously been capable of doing her whole life, and the rest of the family would react this way too. It was only once we realised this was a function of the Alzheimer's that we began to develop patience – a hell of a lot of patience.

I think this was one of the things I struggled with the most: acknowledging that everything that was happening to Mom was not her fault, and not becoming irritated or reactive when she couldn't do something. It was testing, and I admit I failed on many occasions. I had to learn never to say, 'You've already asked me that,' because while she had, she simply didn't remember. Instead, I had to answer the same questions as many times as she asked them, and listen attentively to the same stories as if it was the first time I'd heard them.

It was always worrying when Mom was home alone. We would think, *What if she turns the stove on and forgets about it?* or, *What if she leaves a tap running?* Her behaviour was so unpredictable, her memory so badly affected, that she could forget about what she was doing and move onto something else without realising it. I would often call Mom in the middle of the day just to see what she was doing, to check up on her. We all did.

One weekend afternoon I went over to Mom and Dad's place, aware that Mom had been out most of the day with cousins of ours but expecting her to have returned home. She was nowhere to be seen. I kept calling her mobile but there was no answer, and then I realised her phone was still at home – but she wasn't. I went into full panic mode, thinking the worst. The most likely scenario was that she was out walking, but the idea that she had wandered off alone, with no phone and no sense of direction, was very scary. When Ricky came home from soccer practice, he checked the garage while I drove down to the shops. It was Ricky who found her when he ran up the driveway and saw Mom walking back up the road. She was none the wiser that anything was wrong.

This was another first: the first time we felt we were truly in the midst of a crisis. Things had taken a dramatic turn and we all really felt it. We tried not to show Mom that we were all panicky, as it would have only made things worse for her. Ricky just calmly explained to Mom that when she left the house, she always had to take her keys and phone. It was this episode that led us to put up a whiteboard on the inside of the front door with *Keys* and *Phone* written on it, to prompt Mom when she was leaving the house.

* * *

My brother Greg and sister-in-law Lee-Anne had their first baby the year after Mom was diagnosed. This was the happiest of times for our family. Being the first grandchild for my parents and the first nephew for Ricky and me, the excitement was at an all-time high. As soon as we knew the baby was coming, my family and my sister-in-law's family raced to the hospital to be there for the baby's arrival. It was a moment of pure joy for all of us, and I remember Mom being in great spirits: she was born to be a grandmother and doted on her grandchildren.

By this time, Mom's Alzheimer's was well advanced. She had already stopped driving, so Lee would often walk with the baby to Mom and Dad's house and spend the day with Mom. Lee tried to give Mom as much time with the baby as she could handle, so while they were playing, she would go off into the kitchen and prepare dinner for Mom and Dad. On other days, Lee would take Mom to the shops and they'd do the shopping together, or she'd take Mom back to her house for the day. Mom was pretty amazing with kids and that had not changed. Rather than help Lee with making meals, she preferred to stay out of the kitchen and instead sit with the baby.

During these times, Mom was calm, rarely distressed. We came to understand that it was in Mom's nature to always act as if nothing was ever wrong, never fussing over herself. Reminiscing about this, I now feel there were aspects of the disease and how she felt that Mom concealed from us. I imagine that, in those first few years of symptoms, before the family realised anything was going on, Mom was aware of changes and hid them from us for as long as she possibly could.

I am also conscious that there are things I will never know about what Dad and Ricky experienced. Knowing what I now know, I could have done more, helped more, spent more time with Mom at home, but I adopted an out-of-sight, out-of-mind mentality. I did visit often, though – every few days, taking turns with my brothers on the weekends and weeknights. We had a roster in order to ensure that, for at least three nights during the week, Dad had someone at home with him and Mom. But I still had the freedom to come and go; I could head home and sleep soundly. Dad, on the other hand, was woken up many times by Mom getting up in the middle of the night, confused as to where she was. She would know she needed to go to the bathroom, but where the bathroom was and what she actually needed to do were mysteries to her. She would end up going to the toilet in the middle of the room, sometimes making it as far as the kitchen. Dad often had to clean up, changing clothes and bed linen, his sleep completely interrupted. He would still get up the following day and go to work, never complaining, just dealing with it. His love for Mom was so incredibly strong that irrespective of what she did, he felt it was his duty to care for her in the best way possible. Dad brought new meaning to the vow, 'In sickness and in health.'

The experts, however, tell you that problems can arise when a spouse tries to be the sole carer. Some family carers think they should do everything themselves, and Dad certainly took on an awful lot. It's best for the spouse to discuss how to get more support from other family members and friends, along with professionals, such as those who provide home-care services. This enables the spouse to focus on being with their loved one and giving them emotional support, rather than just physically attending to them all the time. While Dad naturally wanted to take care of Mom, we sensed early on that it would be too much for one person to handle, that it was a big adjustment for Dad. For so long, he and Mom had lived a very happy life together, free of any real issues. They had birthed three children, and moved countries to give my brothers and me a better future. I can only imagine how soul-crushing it was to see the person he loved decline as she did. Those years were harrowing for Dad, and at times things got the better of him. We were all tested in ways unimaginable.

On Mom's birthday each year, while she was still at home, Dad would invite all their friends and family over for afternoon tea. He would make a big fuss over Mom, so much so that everything felt normal. It was wonderful to have those moments among the trauma. Mom would be so happy. One particular birthday, she still looked like her old self, smiling all day. She was in her element, surrounded by all the people she loved and who loved her. She had two grandchildren by then, and there are photos of her holding Greg and Lee's second boy, Dov, of whom she was so proud. It's bittersweet looking at those pictures. You wouldn't think anything was going on, just a normal birthday like any other, Mom celebrating with those close to her. But underneath her smile there was pain, there was confusion and agitation – as there was in all of us.

Friday night is the Jewish Sabbath, which was traditionally hosted at my parents' house each week. For a long time, Mom had typically prepared the Shabbat dinner, which meant collecting the *challah* (the Jewish bread eaten on a Friday night), cooking for the family, setting the table and lighting the Shabbat candles. Now, my Dad and sisters-in-law helped Mom with the cooking, without trying to take over completely, and we would all help set the table and manage the dinner. This was despite domestic duties not being our strong point; in fact, we used to joke that Dad didn't even know where the kitchen was. Suddenly, however, there would be 'too many cooks', and Mom would get agitated, upset that all these people were in *her* kitchen. I think a part of her knew that everyone was there to help her, but she couldn't control how she felt. She also became withdrawn at the dinner table, unable to follow the conversation, feeling left out. We had to make sure she was included, that we talked directly to her and not around her.

As time went on, we noticed more and more people disappearing from Mom's life. Lifelong friends stopped calling and their visits became more infrequent. You would think that all her friends would flock around her, sharing in this life-changing diagnosis. While some friends did, others went the opposite way. It was almost as though, to some, Alzheimer's was contagious. I can understand that it was a hard thing to face, and they didn't know what to do or say, but I believe there is no valid excuse for cutting someone out of your life because you feel uncomfortable with a situation that's out of their control. While we as a family were helped by some of the kindest, most empathetic people, we also experienced some of the most hurtful behaviour, which I don't think I will ever truly understand. I would sometimes find myself justifying other people's actions to Dad, saying they had their own lives, their own children and grandchildren, and we didn't know what else they were dealing with. And I stand by that. But I also know, as someone who has experienced serious illness in my family, that we always have a choice in how we act, and we can always choose kindness towards others.

That's why, when certain people in Mom's life didn't visit her anymore, it was a hard pill to swallow. To the people who claimed it was too painful for them to see Mom like that, I call bullshit. I have a lot of empathy, but not for that. Mom was the one suffering, the one who was losing pieces of herself. The rest of us had one job: to show up and spend time with her. Time is such an important commodity, and at the end of the day, that is all people want and need from one another. It made me sad and angry for Mom. She was suffering enough; she didn't deserve to be abandoned.

Dad's expectations of everyone were just as high as mine. He ruffled some feathers along the way, but only because he cared about Mom and her wellbeing. He needed support because it wasn't possible to look after Mom alone, and it got to the point that Dad felt he had to force people to make arrangements. Love it or hate it, Dad's way of dealing with friends was direct. He would call them and demand that on Monday at 11 a.m., they come and take Mom out.

We were all expected to pull our weight, and it wasn't unreasonable, but I'll admit it was challenging. The boys and I were in a formative time of life: Greg newly married with a baby, Ricky studying and trying to navigate his own relationship, and me at an important junction of my career, about to go from working in a public relations agency to starting my own business. We wanted to live normal lives, but our lives weren't normal anymore, or at least not the normal we were used to. How long was this going to go on for? We had no idea. I hadn't envisaged a life where I'd be looking after Mom because she was unwell at so young an age, and helping to take care of Dad as a result of Mom's situation. It was hard to fathom at times, and selfishly I wanted to just be a normal twenty-something in the prime of my life.

* * *

Luckily, Dad could afford to give my mom the very best care, even if he didn't have the luxury of being at home with her every day. We leant on Jewish Care, an organisation that helps the community in every aspect of life. The challenge was figuring out ways in which Mom could have company during the day and also activities that would stimulate her. But that is the beautiful thing about being part of a community: life can sometimes come full circle. One of the staff members at Jewish Care, Kelly, had gone to school with Greg in South Africa, and we had spent a lot of time together over the years. Kelly is also very talented when it comes to art, and through Jewish

Care she began visiting Mom once a week to paint with her at home. The paintings they did still hang proudly in our homes. The time that Mom spent with Kelly was about so much more than painting, though. It was therapy for the soul. Mom felt empowered, always showing us what she and Kelly had created together. No matter how or what she painted, she was celebrated and encouraged, and that was all that mattered. It was special for both of them, and I am eternally grateful that they found peace and calm in one another.

Kelly describes Mom as being light, carefree, innocent, truly herself in their sessions – there was no doubt that the one-on-one interaction was so beneficial for Mom. One of Kelly's strongest memories of this time is how Mom would talk about the days in South Africa when she was working as a beautician, how much she loved it. Kelly doesn't know if that was true or not, but Mom would speak about it every week, relaying the same information, and Kelly would allow her to retell the story with the same passion and enthusiasm each time. It seemed that Mom had found a commonality between what they did: Kelly as an art teacher would listen to her clients and help them, much like Mom had done as a beautician with clients of her own. This was so confusing. How could Mom remember such intimate details from so many years ago, yet she couldn't remember what she'd eaten for breakfast that morning?

Kelly also remembers a session where Mom wanted to dance, so the two of them got up and danced together. From that day forward, they would put on music that Mom loved, especially Jewish and Hebrew music. Mom had always talked about her love for Yiddishkeit (a Jewish way of life, with Jewish customs and traditions), and she was very proud of her Jewish heritage. She told Kelly about Shabbat dinners and celebrating Jewish holidays, and she showed Kelly her candlesticks.

At one point, Kelly realised that Mom could not tell the difference between any of the paint colours but wouldn't admit it. Rather, Mom would talk about a specific colour with great conviction, or in a roundabout way. Regardless, when it came to the art of painting, she knew exactly what to do. Without any help, she would take the brush, wet it, dip it in the paint and start making brushstrokes. And when she showed us her work, she would do so with immense pride, much like when she talked about her time as a beautician. It was evident that she hadn't felt this kind of achievement since her salon days.

* * *

I've already written about how, over the years following Mom's diagnosis, fewer and fewer of her friends came to visit. Unfortunately, Alzheimer's isn't an illness whereby someone can still function normally, where they're merely being treated and just need some rest until they recuperate. It's a long, arduous illness of decline where things can change at any given time. It means dealing with someone who is losing their memory, who is scared, lonely and confused most of the time. And that is challenging. But there are people who I owe so much to for the time they spent with Mom – two significant people in particular.

When Mom was first diagnosed and still living at home with Dad, my aunt Sheli, the wife of one of Mom's brothers, came to our rescue – she was the guardian angel who became Mom's part-time carer. She would come to the house a few days a week and they would go shopping together, cook together, laugh, sing and dance. By all accounts, the two of them had a ball and were thick as thieves. None of us will ever fully understand the bond that they formed over that time, a bond that remained strong even when Mom moved into an aged-care facility. In the last few years of her life, Mom couldn't engage in conversation, but somehow the two of them would laugh and sing as if they had their own secret language. It was as if Mom was a naughty child getting up to mischief with her best friend. It takes a special kind of person, someone with patience and virtue, to look after someone with Alzheimer's the way Sheli did.

Sheli would arrive in the morning and help Mom to get dressed if she needed assistance. They might go out for lunch, often at Double Bay, where Mom would get her Freezochino and then they'd sit down by the water. They could sit there for hours: Mom was calm around the water and loved watching the children play on the beach. To mix it up, they would spend some days at Rose Bay, sitting by the water there too and going for short walks.

One day Sheli and Mom were baking, consulting an old book in which Sheli would write down all her recipes and paste in ones she'd cut out of magazines; despite being treated with such care, the book was stained with spilt ingredients. Sheli and Mom decided to go out while the goods were in the oven but they forgot to take a key, so they were locked out. I recall them telling me the story, laughing as they described trying to climb through a window. Sheli always made light of any bad situation, and I will forever be indebted to my aunt for bringing fun and light into Mom's life. There was even a day when they were in the study at home and Sheli put the TV music channel on full blast and they danced and sang their hearts out. As Mom's Alzheimer's progressed, it was like she became more childlike. Mom would never have broken into song and dance before, having been more reserved in the past, but now it was as if she had lost all her inhibitions. What a beautiful way to be, to embrace the moment like no-one is watching.

The Long Goodbye

It wasn't all singing and dancing, though. Sheli experienced some confronting times also. Mom had once loved to take a stroll, but over time, walking any distance became less easy. She would come back from a walk sweating and out of breath and would need to go wash. But she would only stay in the shower for two or so minutes – it turned out that once she was in there, Mom wouldn't know what to do or even why she was there. Realising this, Sheli would step in and help her wash. Outside of Dad, Sheli spent the most time with Mom, sharing some of the most joyous moments and also some of the most difficult times with her.

Then there was Caz, another person who had a unique type of patience and acceptance with Mom. Caz has worked for Dad in his dental practice since 1998, a quarter of a century, and basically runs the show, even to this day. She is reliable, hardworking and part of our family. From the moment Mom was unable to do her usual tasks, which meant pretty much everything besides cleaning and filling teeth, Caz stepped up. On some days, instead of working in the practice, Caz would come and spend time with my mom at home. One activity involved organising Mom's photo albums. She had so many photos, covering everything from her wedding day through to ordinary family functions. She and Caz created albums especially for me and each of my brothers, complete with photos from when we were little, from school, our birthdays and holidays, along with notes on the memories contained in each image. I am so thankful for the time Caz spent on those photo albums, something we can all treasure forever.

I hope that Kelly, Sheli and Caz know how significant a role they each played in our lives. There were many days when I was riddled with guilt knowing that Mom was at home without us. So when Kelly, Sheli and Caz started spending time with Mom, they spared us from some of the constant guilt.

* * *

Not long after Mom's diagnosis, I moved home for a couple of months, while I was in-between apartments. It was in the really early days of the Alzheimer's, so Mom was still capable, but nonetheless I got a small taste of what things were like. I was working full-time, so I was usually only home at night and on the weekends, but when I was there, Mom would always want to be in whichever room I was in. She didn't want to be alone, which was understandable, as she would have spent so much time by herself during the day. I began to feel the tension and pressure everyone was under, having to navigate Mom and her dementia. Life became about managing Mom and her needs, and a lot of the fun and laughter which had come naturally before had been lost.

What I witnessed, however, will never compare to what Ricky saw. He has tried to tell me about how upsetting it was being exposed to what was happening to Mom at home, how he watched her dissipate in front of him. He was confronted every day by what he called the 'frightening' spectacle of Mom's short-term memory disappearing: she would be completely oblivious to what she had been asked only moments before. Ricky also came to understand the importance of routine to a person with Alzheimer's. For example, if the cleaner messaged to say she would come on a Tuesday instead of a Monday, this simple change had massive consequences for Mom. She couldn't comprehend it, no matter how much both Ricky and Dad talked her through it, wrote it down, confirmed it, checked it again and double-confirmed it with her the night before and the morning of. She remained upset and confused, totally daunted by this kind of disruption of her routine.

It could not have helped that there was so much change happening all the time. Once we'd begun to manage one stage, another stage would begin. Mom would regress further and we'd learn something new about Alzheimer's that we would need to navigate.

One thing I know for sure is that while I sometimes felt frustrated at the situation, I never once thought, *Why me?* I believe that we are dealt the cards in life that we can handle. I never pity myself or want sympathy from anyone else. More than anything, I just want people to understand the complexities of Alzheimer's, and what happens to someone who has it. Alzheimer's remains a disease with a big stigma attached to it, and most people have no idea how to treat someone with the illness. My wish is for all of us to be kinder to those living with not just Alzheimer's but any disease or disability, that we never treat them differently, nor with any less respect than any other person.

Chapter 6

TRAVEL

Dad's approach to Mom's condition was simple, almost robotic: he would do whatever was required to look after her, and there was nothing and no-one who would get in his way. Dad's expectations of how Mom should be cared for were made known to everyone, and anyone who didn't match up or treat her like an equal, would hear about it. Dad never held back. If he wasn't happy with the way something was being done, or with how Mom's friends were treating her, or with the amount of time Greg, Ricky and I were spending with her, he would openly say so. To him, the only person that mattered was Mom, and he was going to make damn sure that her dignity was protected.

Dad's life had been turned upside down, and while he mostly got on with things, there were times when it all got too much for him and he would lose it at one of us – or all of us. However, he did try to continue doing the 'normal' things he and Mom had done before the diagnosis, and one of these was to travel. Mom and Dad loved to go places, often taking short trips around Australia as well as heading overseas.

I have many fond memories of holidays we went on while I was growing up. Back in South Africa, many July and December school holidays were spent at Umhlanga Beach just north of Durban, Kruger National Park, Sun City, Cape Town, the Drakensburg mountain range and other places across the country. We also twice travelled to Australia before emigrating, with stops in Singapore and Hong Kong. One family holiday was spent in Mauritius, a little piece of paradise in the Indian Ocean. The locals sold all sorts of items on the beach. We bought this one game that had a wooden base and marble balls, the aim of which was to have one ball left on the board. Mom played that game for hours – in Sydney, I'd often arrive home to find Mom playing it, which she did right up until she moved into the first aged-care home. She loved playing card games, too, and was known as the best shuffler in the family. To this day, when we are teaching the kids to shuffle, we always remind them that their *bobba* was the best at this.

After moving to Australia, our family holidays became less frequent, but Mom and Dad still took trips together all the time. Greg and I started going away with our friends in high school, but even as we got older, we still loved going on family holidays. I began to appreciate these getaways even more in my twenties, so when my parents went somewhere, I usually tagged along. When I was living in London for a year after finishing university, I went to meet Mom and Dad in Italy and Paris, and I joined them for a few days on one of their trips to Los Angeles. We also took many trips to Perth to visit my grandparents and cousins. Dad used to say that when he retired, he and Mom would spend all their time travelling.

Another opportunity for travel that Dad never missed was when there was a family *simcha* (celebration). As I've said, maintaining normality was important to Dad in light of the Alzheimer's, and it was also important for him to take part in his brother's *simchas* and for Mom to see her parents. It wasn't a risk to Mom's health to travel, but it was difficult for her to deal with the disorientation, the departure from the usual routine, and the unpredictability of each day away. Mom's moods varied a lot, taking her from calm to depressed, crying and agitated, and it was hard to snap her out of it. So as much as we all wanted to travel to feel normal, some of the trips were hard. But selfishly, I suppose, if we hadn't had the opportunity to travel in those eight years of Mom's illness, I shudder to think how much harder life would have been. Travel kept our sense of adventure alive, and gave us quality time together as a family and with our extended family.

I described earlier how, in 2010, Dad's entire side of the family travelled to Israel for my cousin's wedding. One of Dad's brothers lives in Canada, the other lives in Perth, as do their parents, and we are in Sydney. So it's not often that everyone gets together. In fact, before that trip to Israel, I don't think we'd all been together for over ten years. So it was a pretty special occasion.

In December 2011, six months after we received Mom's diagnosis, another cousin was getting married in Canada, and Mom and Dad were booked to go. I wasn't going to go, but at the last minute my uncle convinced me (his favourite – his only – niece) to attend, and various other family members in Perth were also coming. Looking back at the photos from this trip, Mom looked happy, smiling a lot. When Mom and my aunties Ev and Rose got together, they always had a great time – you would often find them in fits of laughter.

It wasn't all easy in Canada. When Mom woke up, she would have no idea where she was, and it would take her a while to adjust to the new environment. It was at these moments that I really understood the need for routine and familiarity. Back home, Dad would map out Mom's entire week in advance, from when the cleaner would come, to when Sheli or Caz would visit, to the painting sessions with Kelly and the walks with Lynn. It may seem dramatic and overblown, but it was vital Mom had some sense of control over her life.

Despite the disorientation, Mom seemed to handle the trip to Canada well. It's hard to know how she was really feeling, but she seemed to find ways to manage and compensate. This was still early in the progression of the disease, when Mom could function OK and there were still plenty of good days.

On this trip, we spent a week in Edmonton, where an uncle and aunt of mine live. Edmonton is like a country town, although it's not that small. One of the main hotels is situated in the West Edmonton Mall, and that's where we stayed. On New Year's Eve we had a family dinner and afterwards we found a bar that was throwing a new year party. Mom and Dad, my uncle and aunt from Perth, my cousin Danny and I all joined in, and we danced the night away. Mom seemed to be having the time of her life, and in that moment it felt like everything had gone back to normal. What Alzheimer's?!

* * *

Shortly after the Canada trip, we took the first of two trips to Hawaii. Mom and Dad loved the place and had been there a few times already, often staying at the same hotel, so there was a level of familiarity we thought might provide some comfort to Mom.

That first trip was one of the best family holidays I can remember. Greg might not agree – travelling with an eighteen-month-old had its challenges, and there were many times he was stuck in a hotel room trying to get his baby to sleep. But I loved being away with my oldest nephew. We went to Waikiki in Honolulu, and my uncle and aunt from Canada also stayed there for a few days. Dad, my uncle and aunt, and I would get up early in the morning to go for a run or otherwise exercise, while Mom would say in bed, which wasn't unusual. On our way back to the hotel, Dad would stop at a Starbucks to get Mom her Frappuccino (the local version of her beloved Freezochinos back home), and she couldn't have been happier. Our days were spent basking in the sun at the pool, or on the beach out the front of our hotel. We drifted in the ocean on li-los for hours on end. Mom was never really the adventurous kind, so when we went jet-skiing she was only too happy to stay at the hotel or go shopping.

The second trip to Hawaii about two years later was very different. This time, Mom and Dad were going for a fortnight and I joined them for the first week of the trip.

We flew into Waikiki and stayed at the Moana Surfrider hotel on the beachfront, where my parents had stayed many times before. Mom was still living at home but her Alzheimer's had progressed, and I've since questioned whether or not this trip should have happened. But these holidays were part of Dad's coping mechanism, and who was I to argue with that?

Mom was quite difficult to deal with, although through no fault of her own. It just wasn't a good week. Perhaps the disease had progressed more than we realised. Whatever the reason, Mom was extremely out of sorts, her mood was low, and she became very disorientated. We couldn't leave her alone – she was too confused and would get teary and upset if we tried to do something without her. On the previous trip, she'd been only too happy to stay in bed while we went running, but not this time. It was as if she'd lost all confidence in herself.

One day we met a family from Melbourne at the pool. Dad can talk to anyone, so he started chatting to them. Back in the day, Mom would have been yapping away too, but now she wouldn't say anything, and Dad finally had to explain what was going on. Someone who wasn't aware of the situation may have thought that Mom was being rude, but it wasn't her – it was the Alzheimer's. We fared no better when our two families went out for dinner one night and the restaurant turned out to be quite loud.

Mom just couldn't deal with it, being unable to take part in the conversation. That made it hard for Dad to socialise because he was keeping one eye on Mom. Spending time with another family was not an unusual situation, but because of the Alzheimer's it was extremely hard – on us, on them, and on Mom.

Mom loved to shop, but Dad loved it more. He delights in giving gifts. When my brothers and I were kids, he would bring home new toys for us all the time. But after returning from a drive down to the outlet shops in Waikiki for a morning of shopping, where we'd bought Mom a fair amount of stuff, she became angry and upset. She was again like a little kid who wasn't getting their way, and we couldn't quite understand what had caused it. It later transpired that she was angry because she believed that my dad had bought all that stuff for 'some woman' and nothing for her. The woman in question turned out to be me – Mom had forgotten who I was, and couldn't connect the dots. This was one of the first times that I can remember Mom forgetting who I was. It was both utterly devastating that my own mother wasn't able to recognise me, and at the same time it was also slightly funny and brought a sense of relief – we finally understood her behaviour on the trip.

A few days later, Mom was still in a bad mood, acting irrationally, being difficult to deal with. Dad and I tried to make light of the situation but nothing really worked. She'd barely talk to us. There was the odd good time – going out to dinner, hanging around the pool – but mostly there was just this heaviness. When we flew from Oahu to Kauai for a few days, Mom got a bit better, although she was still very clingy with Dad. Dad and I wanted to go on a helicopter ride together over some volcanoes, but we couldn't leave Mom on her own, so we had to go individually.

As soon as I left Hawaii, Mom's entire mood apparently lifted and she was a different person. She began smiling again, her mood was lighter, and she and Dad enjoyed a great second week together. It really did seem that Mom had mistaken me for some other woman and had resented me being around, feeling that I was impeding her and taking her husband's attention, and she wasn't able to get past it until I was gone. It was a fictitious story she had told herself and then come to believe.

Looking back, I have to laugh about that situation, as it was all part of the complex disease that is Alzheimer's. I couldn't work out what was going on in Mom's mind because her memory had been compromised and she couldn't express what she was thinking. But I'll never regret those opportunities to travel with my mom, no matter how difficult those times could be.

Chapter 7

SIMCHAS
(Celebrations)

When Greg married Lee in 2007, Mom was already showing early signs of Alzheimer's. They were subtle, not enough to make us question her behaviour too much, but in hindsight they were there.

Greg's wedding was a huge deal. He was the first of us three children to get married, and we were overjoyed, as was Lee's family. We were involved in every aspect of the wedding, from planning meetings to carrying out some of the decorative tasks. A few weeks before the event, we were all at Lee's parents' house, helping with the preparations. I remember all of us sitting around the dining-room table, joking, laughing, so excited about the wedding. But Mom wasn't herself. There was a sense of sadness about her, and it seemed as though she was there under duress, whereas usually she would be the first to offer a helping hand. At the time we thought she probably felt out of place – it was her son's wedding after all, yet the attention was focused on the bride.

On other occasions, when Mom accompanied Lee and her mum to different appointments, she would hold onto the back of Lee's mum's top while they were walking and basically follow her around. It didn't make sense at the time but no-one made a big deal about it. And these minor incidents were all forgotten when the weekend of the wedding came around.

When Ricky's wedding to Lauren took place in December 2013, however, Mom was well and truly affected by Alzheimer's. She still very much looked like herself, and often graced us with her big, beautiful smile. But we could tell she was struggling but was holding on for the occasion. Her desire to see another son walk down the aisle would have been hugely motivating.

Mom needed to buy a dress for the wedding that matched the colour chosen for the bridal party, but shopping was difficult for her. The process of getting that dress was a painful one. Firstly, it was hard to find an outfit in the right colour, but taking Mom to the shop and having her try on different options was even more challenging. We had to go into the changing room with her and help her out of her clothes and into the dress. That was invasive enough, a grown woman needing to be undressed and dressed, but she also didn't trust herself to make a decision, being completely unsure as to what looked nice. She was reliant on other people to make these decisions, and if we were uncertain, she would get upset. Her mood was another factor: we had to be lucky enough to get Mom on a good day, and we never knew when that would be.

Fortunately, not long before the wedding, Dad decided to take a trip with Mom to Melbourne to see some family and friends, and while they were there, one of Mom's cousins found a dress for her. Truthfully, I was relieved. I used to love shopping with Mom, but Alzheimer's had taken all the fun out of it. It took a lot of patience and, admittedly, that was something I often lacked.

Wedding planning was not an easy task either, considering Mom's condition. Ricky wanted to include her as much as possible, but he couldn't allocate her a task because she simply wouldn't have been able to do it. Everyone just ended up trying their best to make sure she wasn't left out. Lauren would take colour samples and photos of decor samples over to Mom to involve her in the decision-making, although Mom would sometimes just stare at them, not really understanding what they were.

By the day of Ricky and Lauren's wedding, Mom was a different person to who she'd been at Greg's wedding. There were moments where she was dancing happily, and times when she looked confused and sad. You could almost see the deterioration of her soul. I believe Mom knew she wasn't well, that she was declining, but she managed to hold herself together because she so badly wanted to be at her best for the wedding. Once it was over, however, she quickly began falling apart, regressing further and further due to the disease. Soon, the person she had been at Ricky's wedding was no longer there. A little spark in her had gone out.

A few weeks after the wedding, while all of our extended family was still in town, we threw a celebration for my grandfather's ninetieth birthday. This was a milestone – to be surrounded by his three sons, almost all of his grandchildren, and his great-grandchildren was truly something special. It should have been a happy occasion for everyone, and mostly it was. Except for Mom, who was so unhappy that day. The sad reality of Alzheimer's had taken away Mom's ability to enjoy family celebrations. When the attention wasn't focused on her, she became angry and sad.

Still, we never stopped celebrating things through the years Mom had Alzheimer's. At the time it could feel arbitrary to do so, because Mom had deteriorated so much, but it was important that we acknowledge and celebrate each other, including Mom. That is one of the beautiful things you learn in such situations: to find joy in hard times. That's why, every year on Mom's birthday, regardless of how she was doing, we celebrated. Dad would always make a speech, thanking everyone for being there, but not mentioning Alzheimer's. For a few hours, we could switch off from reality and try to enjoy the occasion for what it was.

When Mom moved into an aged-care facility, we continued to make a fuss over every birthday and Mother's Day, partly because we never knew when it would be the last one. We would bring cake, sing 'Happy Birthday' and make memories with the grandchildren. It was especially important to Dad that we came together for these occasions. He pushed so hard for this that I would wonder if he was in denial about the severity of Mom's situation or if he simply wanted things to be normal where possible. Either way, we made the most it. I knew it then and I appreciate it even more now, how Dad's need for Mom to be treated as a human being, with full respect, was his number-one priority.

* * *

Mom's fiftieth birthday party took place a few years before everything started to unravel. It's the last milestone birthday I can remember where everything was 'normal'. We had it at Mom and Dad's place on the North Shore, and all of her friends and family were there. Dad put on one of my corduroy jackets in an attempt to mimic the suede suit he wore at their wedding – it must have been trendy at the time – and played guitar and sang to Mom. Dad doesn't have a musical bone in his body, so it was disastrous. But that's Dad – he's never cared about what other people think. I am sure a part of Mom cringed at the sight of Dad, but another part of her would have been laughing along. It was the sentiment behind it all that Mom would have appreciated.

After that event, all of my memories of Mom's birthdays are associated with Alzheimer's. As she became more confused, we worked out that Mom was better in smaller groups, where the focus could be on her – especially on a day like her birthday. It also became clear that celebrating birthdays, anniversaries and Mother's Days was very important to the rest of us. While we needed to learn more and more about what was happening to Mom, we also needed, as much as we could, to go about life as we always had.

Dad's life had taken its own beating, so we also made sure we celebrated Father's Day and his own birthday in a big way. For Dad's sixtieth, which coincided with the Jewish Passover, we decided to have the party in Perth, combining the two events so Dad could celebrate them both with his parents, brothers and their children – there is no doubt that Dad would have loved for Mom to be there, but unfortunately it was too hard. We have family in Perth who live on what has always been referred to as 'The Farm', which is not a real farm but rather a big property where various fruits were grown, and which was perfect for the occasion. My uncle organised a huge jumping castle – one of those ones where you put on a sumo suit and wrestle or play-fight inside – and everyone had lots of fun.

Every once in a while I'd stop and remember that Mom was not with us, that she was missing the fun while we were all missing her. Dad, more than anyone, would have felt the void of her absence. Yet he somehow managed to keep smiling, to keep going. He had become very good at compartmentalising his life into time with Mom and time without Mom. Still, as enjoyable as that trip was, there was an underlying sense of sadness that Mom was not with us. The idea that one can experience joy and sadness simultaneously was never truer for me than at that time. Until then, I'd always thought those two feelings were mutually exclusive.

* * *

My thirtieth birthday did involve Mom, and this brought predictable challenges. My family went for a quiet dinner at our favourite local restaurant. We have this tradition in our family where we always write each other's birthday cards at the dinner table. It started many years ago, probably because we would always forget to buy a card in advance of the birthday and end up rushing out to get one on the way to the celebration. This night was no different. Anyway, I was reading my cards and opening my gifts at the table when Mom started getting teary and upset because no-one had bought her any gifts. All she could see was that 'someone else' was being given gifts by Dad and, in an echo of Hawaii, that immediately set her off.

Mom and Dad were married on Dad's birthday, and so 2 April was usually a double celebration. But my brothers and I would often forget about the anniversary until the eleventh hour, then hurriedly prepare to mark it. But as Mom declined, it felt more important to continue acknowledging such milestones. We never knew how many more years we would have to celebrate anything.

* * *

Yom Tovs (Jewish holidays) were by far the most confronting occasions for us. Yom Tov is where we take time off from the wider world to honour Jewish history and traditions, and most importantly come together as a family to celebrate. Growing up in a Jewish home, there's a distinct feeling you get around the time of these festivals, because your house becomes so busy in the weeks leading up to them; in particular, there's a lot of cooking going on. We'd come home from school or university or work and the house would be in *balagan* (chaos). Multiple things would be cooking at once, and different aromas would be floating through the house. Special platters and dishes that were only to be used for Jewish festivals would come out of the cupboard, before being stowed away again for the remainder of the year. Extra tables and chairs would be laid out so as to seat everyone in one room.

When Mom could no longer participate, a sense of loss enveloped my family. Mom had been the driving force behind our Yiddishkeit, but as the centre of our world, of our Jewish traditions, she could no longer lead the way. It felt wrong to be celebrating without her. I hated the fact that she was sitting in a home by herself, unable to be with her family, especially as I knew how much the Jewish festivals meant to her. So I would always go and see her on the Jewish festival days and spend time with her.

My brothers have been exceptional at keeping everything going, despite feeling this loss. I am aware, too, of the importance of maintaining our traditions; I will never stop them. My brothers' children have brought a new sense of fun and meaning to the Jewish festivals – it's amazing to watch them take part and make new memories. And to this day, whichever house we go to, the family acknowledges Mom when welcoming everyone. It's touching to know that no-one has or will ever forget Mom, that she is still deeply etched in our past, present and future.

Chapter 8

HEALTHY BRAIN AGEING

After Mom's official diagnosis, the reality of her condition began to set in. The more books we read, the more doctors and dementia specialists we spoke to, the bleaker the outlook appeared. There was no cure, not a glimmer of hope. Yes, some clinical trials were being done, but the doctors were clear that there was no concrete proof anything would work. We would have done anything to help Mom, but we were at a loss.

Over the first few years, there were so many things about Mom that changed. She would have these moments, sometimes stretching across days, where she seemed so normal, her old self, and I would think to myself, *Maybe they got the diagnosis wrong.* But these times were fleeting and she would inevitably plunge back into the depths of Alzheimer's. I've always lived by the saying, 'Where there's a will, there's a way,' but in this instance it was completely out of my hands. There was simply nothing I could do to 'cure' Mom. I could only watch her slowly slip away.

Some of these feelings were overpowering. On my part, I felt an overwhelming sense of helplessness, which is a feeling that doesn't sit comfortably with me. I have a tendency to always want to be in control, to believe that if you work at what you want hard enough, you can control your destiny. But here I was, faced with something I had no influence over. I often thought if we could stop Mom from drinking anything with sugar or aspartame – key ingredients in her daily Freezochinos and Pepsi Maxes – or if she had a personal trainer and increased the amount of exercise she was doing, maybe she would improve. Dad – who has a good medical understanding – would read and learn about Alzheimer's. We spoke to medical professionals and professors, and all the reading and research pointed to physical activity and healthy eating as factors in addressing the development of dementia, with the capacity to potentially slow the disease's progress and lessen its symptoms.

We considered many ways to keep Mom active. We attempted a personal trainer but she was very resistant.

We dabbled in Pilates. For a few months, we even went to Pilates classes with Mom as a family. It didn't last very long. We also tried tennis for a while, which was probably the most successful. She was happy to do something physical if we were with her, but not on her own with a trainer. Walking was the most consistent form of exercise Mom would do, until she could no longer manage to walk far distances.

It's still hard to accept, but sometimes I had moments when I was angry with Mom, thinking, *How could she let this happen?* I needed to blame someone; someone had to take responsibility. Really, I think I was angry at myself for not being able to help.

* * *

It was in 2012, about a year after Mom was diagnosed, that I saw a segment on a TV morning show in which PJ Lane from the Centre for Healthy Brain Ageing (CHeBA) was talking about the launch of an initiative called the Dementia Momentum. The date of the launch was significant as it was three years to the day since PJ's father had passed away from Alzheimer's. I was immediately compelled to investigate CHeBA, so I jumped on the website and found the contact details for Heidi Douglass, CHeBA's head of communications. I reached out to Heidi –

working in communications myself, I thought I could use my network and expertise to help her efforts – which sparked the beginning of a meaningful relationship with an organisation I know I will be connected to for life.

When I first met Heidi, I straightaway felt a sense of calmness and understanding. I was met with empathy, not sympathy, which was so important. She was compassionate, and committed to making a difference. In Heidi, I recognised someone who was doing something about Alzheimer's, and I wanted to join her. What especially drew me to CHeBA was that their research into brain ageing was not only about treating Alzheimer's but also had a preventative element. This appealed to me because, while I was dealing with Mom's diagnosis, I had the lingering thought that this could be hereditary: *What if I develop Alzheimer's one day?* I told my brothers about the organisation and we all signed on as CHeBA fitness ambassadors, with the aim of fundraising for research into healthy brain ageing, taking part in media opportunities, and raising awareness of dementia through sport and fitness initiatives. It felt like the perfect fit.

The connection with CHeBA gave me a whole new sense of meaning and purpose. It was also the beginning of my personal campaign for healthy living. I couldn't sit on the sidelines and do nothing. This was my way of giving back, of trying to make a difference, if not for Mom then for people who might develop Alzheimer's in the future and their families. Over the years I've worked with CHeBA, I've witnessed that the work they do to raise funds for research and encourage education is unfaltering. In CHeBA, I found my tribe: people who were going through the same thing I was, and who understood me without any explanation. Friends and family can be supportive, but sometimes you need people around you who just get it because they have lived it.

* * *

PJ joined CHeBA after his dad, Don Lane, the well-known talk-show host and singer, passed away in 2009 at the age of seventy-five, and his commitment to the organisation since then hasn't wavered. Don was diagnosed with Alzheimer's in his early seventies and PJ gave up an international professional basketball career to care for his dad. To be that selfless says a lot about a person. It reminds me of my Dad: there wasn't a thing he wouldn't do for Mom.

PJ started noticing signs of Alzheimer's in 1998, when his dad did little things PJ thought were a bit odd. PJ remembers arguing with him about the colours on a basketball team's jersey. Don was convinced they were green and yellow, but the jersey was actually white, which PJ tried to point out to him. In the end, Don gave up and just walked off.

On another occasion, Don was driving a car in which PJ was a passenger, and he would accelerate then brake, accelerate then brake, repeatedly. When PJ questioned him about it, he couldn't explain it; instead, he got really angry.

Another thing PJ noticed, beginning in 2001, was his dad's balance, which became progressively worse. Don was still really mentally sharp at that point. He would tell stories, remember details and people's names. His body started giving way before his mind did.

PJ and his dad then travelled to America together, where PJ discovered Don was noticeably less active than usual, spending a lot of time in front of the TV. He was also making various mistakes due to basic forgetfulness. Making matters worse, Don's driving was now a major concern. He would drift off into another lane, and PJ had to draw a dot on the windshield to help Don steer straight. PJ thought it might be a neurological issue rather than a cognitive one, as Don was still so with it. Back then, like most of us, PJ didn't know much about Alzheimer's. Don and his friends used to make jokes about the disease. Someone would say 'What was I talking about again?' and another person would answer 'Alzheimer's'.

When PJ was in Greece pursuing his basketball career, he would come back to Australia to visit his dad, and on these trips he noticed that Don had trouble using the phone. Remembering numbers was difficult for him, so PJ wrote the important ones down. He also labelled the TV remote as Don was having difficulty with that too. Don was still very coherent and looked healthy, but his balance was even more problematic, and he'd started losing weight because he kept forgetting to eat. PJ was worried because Don lived by himself. In 2008, PJ finally moved his dad into a low-care facility, which prompted more of a decline. Don started making less and less sense when he spoke, drifting off in mid-conversation. He would get into arguments with other residents, which led to him being moved into a high-care facility in January 2009.

Soon Don was in a wheelchair, having lost his ability to walk, and he couldn't form the words or sentences to articulate what he was trying to say. Don also started forgetting who PJ was – he knew the two were emotionally connected, but that was it. The decline was severe, with Don passing within twenty months of being moved into the low-care place.

PJ was in denial right up until the end. He believed so strongly there was something he could do. He was adamant a cure would be found and they'd be able to stop the disease. Even when his dad stopped eating, PJ would still go to McDonald's and buy a thickshake to get some calories into his father. This was about a month before Don passed and PJ was sure he was onto something: if he could get his dad to eat, he could prolong his life. And he kept trying to make Don's environment as nice as possible. PJ recorded a South Sydney Rugby League game – Don liked sport – and he kept playing it to his father. Don kept rewatching it, unaware it was the same game.

When a loved one with Alzheimer's passes, it's a hard thing for those left behind to grasp. On the one hand, you feel like you have lost the battle, while on the other hand you know that your loved one is now free. Either way, the guilt you feel about not being able to save your loved one, about whether you could have done something more, never really leaves you. The sense of defeat keeps running through you, leaving you bewildered.

A conversation with anyone who has been personally affected by dementia is always about education and awareness. So many people have little to no understanding of what dementia is and why it's so prevalent, which makes it very hard to raise money for research. Only through lived experience can you know exactly how much of an issue the disease is; how its impact extends way beyond the person who has been diagnosed with it; the extent of the mental, physical, emotional and financial toll it can take on a family; the need for carers and specialised care options; the cost to society. In terms of the mortality rate, dementia has overtaken most other diseases and illnesses, affecting over 400,000 Australians every year, yet it is still not perceived as significant.

PJ was CHeBA's first ambassador and after ten years he is still carrying the torch for the organisation. In 2022 he ran the Blackmores Half Marathon to raise money for CHeBA, and the following year he doubled down on his effort and tackled the Sydney Marathon, raising $20 000. I find it incredible to be surrounded by people like PJ who are so passionate about this cause and continue to show up for the future of healthy brain ageing. I know from direct experience that it's not easy caring for someone with Alzheimer's; it's confronting, and at times infuriating. That's why I admire PJ so much, because of what he sacrificed to care for his father. Almost fifteen years later, PJ still honours his dad through his ambassador work with CHeBA and through fundraising events where he can continue to share his dad's story and love for entertaining.

* * *

Soon after joining CHeBA a year or so after my mom was diagnosed in 2012, I wanted to contribute to its efforts, to raise money and feel like I was doing something for Mom. So my brothers and I created a fun run from Bondi to Bronte, and we invited all of our friends and family members to tackle the route with us. It was a beautiful sunny day as we took over a section of grass at the northern end of Bondi, and spirits were high. Mom was there too, and she was in a good mood that day. In fact, I still think about the event with elation. I think it was the first time I publicly acknowledged Mom's diagnosis. More importantly, we were all focused on running, walking, enjoying each other's company and raising money for CHeBA. The power of community is something I have never taken for granted, and I feel immensely privileged to have grown up being supported by mine. I look back at the photos from this day with so much joy, remembering the feeling that we were making a difference.

After the success of that day, I wanted to do more. Fitness is a huge part of my life and I love training and a little bit of friendly competition. I approached Chris, the owner of 98 Gym where I train, with an idea to raise money in a team-style gym event, and he got onboard immediately. I invited other gyms to put together teams of five people with a minimum entry fee, and asked everyone to raise money for their team, with everything to be donated directly to CHeBA. The energy on the day was high, the music was pumping, and everyone went all in. The session was tough, and when we finished there were sweaty bodies lying everywhere, breathless but with a feeling of achievement. We raised over $4000 that day.

I am not a fan of public speaking, but I remember standing up in front of everyone before we started and telling them why I was doing this and what it meant.

At that moment, I realised that when you speak about something that means so much to you, it's actually easy to get up in front of an audience. You realise that people are inherently kind and will almost always get behind you. All you have to do is ask.

* * *

It terrifies me to think that what happened to my Mom, at such a young age, could eventually happen to me. But I don't want to live my life in fear. Instead, I make healthy choices every day: eating for my brain and general wellbeing, staying active and keeping my brain firing. I am not taking any chances, because I've seen how devastating Alzheimer's is, not only for the person experiencing it but for their family, the people who care for them. I wouldn't wish it upon anyone, and that's why, for me, healthy brain ageing is absolutely a priority.

In 2023, towards the end of summer, I was down in Bondi for the annual WipeOut Dementia event, another incredible initiative of CHeBA in partnership with the property industry. It was a warm Friday morning as I watched the surfers waxing their boards and getting ready to paddle out for their heats. As I stood on the shoreline, I found myself talking to one of the CHeBA researchers, someone I hadn't met before. We got to talking about Mom and her life, and how important Alzheimer's research is, and the widespread lack of knowledge about how to treat someone with Alzheimer's. The researcher agreed with me that the lack of understanding around this disease desperately needs to be addressed.

If there is one thing that Mom instilled in me above any other it was to always give back to your community and to be charitable. It was innate in her; she didn't have to tell me how, she showed me how and if there is one thing I'd want to impart from Mom, it would be the encouragement to serve others.

Chapter 9

MOVING DAY – THE FIRST HOME

We had always known that moving Mom into a care facility was inevitable; what we didn't know was when that would happen. Dad certainly resisted it for as long as he could. He felt that, as her husband, it was his responsibility to look after Mom. But over time, managing Mom at home had become significantly more difficult. Home for Dad began to lose its sense of comfort and calm, transforming into a harsh place of no respite, filled with constant reminders of the painful reality of Alzheimer's.

It was no longer a place I loved to come back to, either. It was tense there, and there was always something that needed attention: looking after Mom, cleaning up, helping

Dad with other chores, paying the bills. As Mom's ability kept diminishing, so too did the feeling of home.

As I explained earlier, sequencing becomes challenging for a person with Alzheimer's. Mom would get up to do something and within seconds forget what it was. She'd walk into the laundry and not be able to work out what she was doing there – or for that matter, what the room was for. Even the sight of the washing machine wouldn't always trigger her memory, or if it did, she'd forget how to switch it on. When Mom had travelled to South Africa to see Bobba, she'd stuck some instructions on the washing machine, as none of us knew how to use it. Now, she wasn't capable of following the instructions she herself had written.

Mom's recurring urinary tract infections were another major problem. Dad installed a bidet in the bathroom to help make sure Mom stayed clean, but using such things doesn't come easily to a person with Alzheimer's. Dad would also need to check that Mom had brushed her teeth properly, washed her hands after using the toilet, showered properly – her health and hygiene were always top of mind. Mom became more and more inactive, especially when she stopped walking as much. She had put on a lot of weight and her physicality declined. Her appetite increased significantly, but that wasn't the only reason she started to put on weight – she'd literally forget she'd just eaten and would ask for more food. This also led to her snoring quite loudly, preventing Dad from sleeping; he'd have to move into the spare room.

After that second Hawaii trip, Dad knew he couldn't go on like he had been. The trip was the catalyst for making the decision to move Mom into a home. Dad simply couldn't manage her anymore – nor should he have had to. It was actually important for Dad to create a separation between being carer and spouse, as the experts had advised him. The dual roles were not healthy for him, and furthermore, staying at home was not in Mom's best interest anymore. Still, the decision to move her into a facility that specifically cared for people with Alzheimer's wasn't easy. We all felt like we were giving up and passing on the responsibility to care for her. Mom was so young, still in her fifties, so the idea of her going into an 'old-age' facility was hard to accept.

When it came to finding a place we could settle my mom into, we were fortunate in coming across what felt more like a 'home' than a 'facility', which put us all at ease. It is not lost on me how lucky and privileged we were that we could move Mom into a place like that, which came at a significant cost. Dad got some advice from a financial planner who had a contact who knew the system and could help Dad fill out the mountain of paperwork involved. Without that help, the whole process would have been so much more confusing. People who have found themselves in a similar situation have told me how hard it was for them to navigate Australia's complex aged-care system. The truth is, it's not set up to deal effectively with dementia, which only ends up making an already difficult situation that much tougher.

The place we found, which specifically catered to dementia patients, was a big house in which each resident had their own bedroom and bathroom. The house was situated in the North Shore, close to where we had lived for most of our time in Sydney, although it was quite a distance from where we now resided in the eastern suburbs. Ironically, it had not been that long ago that Mom and Dad had moved to the eastern suburbs to be closer to my brothers and me, but now Mom was heading back north.

We never told Mom she was going to be leaving her home and her husband to live somewhere she would be looked after by strangers. How would that conversation have gone? How would she have been able to make sense of that? It was unfathomable. Trying to explain it to her would have only upset her, and us too. We tried to approach the situation as practically as we could, although with very mixed emotions. The specialists advised us how to approach moving day, which was to not tell her she was moving. To make the transition easier, in the evening before we left, they gave her a sedative. We followed their advice. We were doing this for the sake of Mom's care, even though, perhaps selfishly, it was going to make life easier for us too.

* * *

It was a Sunday, and Dad had arranged for him and Mom to have lunch with my aunty Sheli and her husband, Mom's brother. To Mom, it was like any other day – she was none the wiser about what was about to happen. The four of them sat and ate lunch at a familiar restaurant overlooking the harbour, and there was no reason for her to suspect anything.

While Mom was out, my brothers and I packed up her things and made our way to Mom's new home. We set up her room – the biggest in the house – making sure there were lots of familiar items that she could identify with. We unpacked her clothes and put them in the closet, and laid out her toiletries and hair dryer in the bathroom – all the little things she would use daily. We put a blanket on her bed that she had slept with in winter, and arranged family photos, and later Dad put some chocolates in the drawer next to her bed. We wanted to make her new home feel like *home*.

My memory of this day is scattered. Part of me believes that, when she was finally brought to the place, Mom was distraught and kept asking to go back to her real home.

But Dad remembers Mom being very calm, not fighting what was happening. It's likely his recollection is more accurate. Mom was unaware of what was happening because her memory was sadly that far gone. In this instance, however, that served as a good thing.

We stayed with Mom all of that afternoon and through dinnertime, then a nurse came and gave Mom a sedative to help with any anxiety, to calm her for a smooth transition. We didn't make a big fuss about leaving as we didn't want to give Mom a reason to panic – we just left. I could sense she felt something was happening, but the reality is that was probably more about the guilt I was feeling than what Mom was actually going through. Driving home, I swung back and forth between the guilt and relief, experiencing really mixed emotions. I finally had to admit I felt some comfort in knowing she was now in the hands of people who were qualified to care for her and provide her with stimulation, people who weren't as emotionally involved as family members could be.

When Dad was driving home, he started to cry so uncontrollably that he had to pull over. It had just hit him that his wife, who he had shared a bed and a home with for thirty-seven years, was no longer going to go to sleep beside him, that he would wake up alone for the first time since they were married. He called me, wanting to be picked up, as he didn't think he could drive home in that state, but eventually he calmed down enough to do it. That broke me: my dad, the one who had always held everything together, had fallen apart over the love of his life. He and Mom were now apart, not by choice but because of awful circumstances, and it was unbearable. Dad still gets choked up when he recalls that first night alone, the feeling of complete emptiness. And he probably always will – the loneliness may never fade.

The new home wasn't close to where we all lived, so we couldn't just pop around the corner to see Mom on the spur of the moment. You needed at least three spare hours, half of which would be spent driving there and back. This played on my mind: when and how often would I get to see Mom? Like the rest of my family, I was working full-time, so that only left weekday evenings and weekends, and to be truthful, sometimes I just wanted to wake up on a Saturday or Sunday morning and have the day to myself. And what would happen on Friday nights? Having a Shabbat without Mom would be so strange; never in our lives had Mom not been there for a Shabbat dinner. Would it be unsettling if we brought Mom home for it? Did we have to return her to the home afterwards or could she stay with us overnight? There was a lot to consider, and then to reconsider.

It actually didn't take long for Mom to settle in. That was the ironic thing about the whole situation: it was heartbreaking to move Mom, but with her memory lapsing so much, she soon forgot about her old home. After a while she stopped asking to be returned there, and as tough as that was to fathom, it was also a relief. Dad, though, continued to struggle. He often wanted to bring Mom home for a Sunday lunch with the family. I never knew if this was a good idea or not: would she suddenly remember this was her old home and not want to leave? Would it confuse her too much? We did bring Mom home on a few occasions and it was OK, but eventually it became clear, even to Dad, that it wasn't doing Mom any good.

Dad did go and visit Mom every day. He would work most days until 1 p.m., drive straight to the home and spend the entire afternoon with her. Some days he would take her to the local shops for lunch, or he would take her for a walk around the nearby streets, or simply sit in the garden with her. And on the weekends, he would stay there all day. Mom would have a shower before dinner, and Dad would use the opportunity to go for a run before they ate together. Mom had begun sleeping more than usual so she would go to bed pretty early; it wasn't until she was asleep that Dad would leave.

When Dad visited, Mom would follow him around, refusing to leave his side. She may have been confused and losing her memory, but Dad still felt familiar and comfortable to her. She would even follow him into the bathroom, causing him to joke that he never had any privacy.

There were less than ten people living at the home, which was more of a boutique place than your regular aged-care home, and the carers, who were known as 'homemakers', were truly amazing. Mom loved music and dancing, so in the mornings the staff would put on a song and dance with her. She was happiest when dancing, as it gave her a sense of freedom, being something she could do without really thinking. Mom was very well cared for, not least because the staff were the heart and soul of this home, as they are at similar places. They were there 24/7, devoting so much of their time and energy to the residents, doing a job that so many others won't or can't do. It really does take a special person to dedicate their life to the wellbeing of others: cooking for them, feeding them, taking them to the toilet, doing activities with them. I don't believe enough credit is given to those who do this work.

Having said this, carers at aged-care homes are often limited by the resources available to them. At the end of the day, homes like the one in which Mom was cared for are a business, and they can become under-resourced. Looking after dementia patients means providing care and assistance twenty-four hours a day, which is hugely demanding for all involved. After seeing what the carers do for dementia patients, their care is something I will be forever grateful for. It is a tedious and sometimes unrewarding role, but they perform it with so much care and kindness in sometimes very challenging situations.

* * *

One weekday afternoon, I was in a meeting with a client when my phone rang, and it kept ringing. When I finally checked it, there were several missed calls from Dad, and I knew something was wrong. I wrapped up the meeting as quickly as I could and called Dad, who told me to get to the home right away. Something was wrong with Mom: she was semiconscious, and it didn't look good. When I finally got there, I ran to her room, where I found Dad and my brothers. Mom was staring into space, looking comatose, with nothing behind her eyes. Some doctors told us they didn't know what was going on, only that Mom might not see it through, that this could be the end.

It was surreal. We had known that Mom's life was going to be cut short, but not this short. That morning she'd been fine, and then out of nowhere this had happened. We sat there on her bed for hours, but her condition didn't change. I felt a lump in my throat. Was this really it? I couldn't hold back the tears; none of us could. Everything was happening so fast, yet time was standing still. At some point, one of the nurses said Mom might have a urinary tract infection, and she was put on an antibiotic to see if she would improve.

We all went home that night in disbelief, not knowing what tomorrow would bring, whether Mom would make it through the night. We started changing our collective mindset, preparing for the worst. What if this was *the* day?

The next day, Mom was back to normal. It was indeed a urinary tract infection that had gone untreated, and Mom made a full recovery. Nonetheless, that episode completely messed with us. A part of us had been preparing for the worst, because we had to. We hadn't wanted our minds to go there, but it was the reality we were facing. And then, suddenly, everything was back to the 'new normal' and we again had to readjust. What we didn't know then was that it wouldn't be the last time we would have to deal with something like this.

By now, Mom was unable to communicate very well, so we became her voice, making sure that all the important things were attended to, ensuring that she was washed and dressed, and had her hair and make-up done every day. We wanted to maintain Mom's dignity, have her cared for in the way she had once cared for herself, when she'd always looked immaculate. She used to take great pride in her appearance, and that wasn't to be neglected just because she couldn't do it for herself anymore.

* * *

The Long Goodbye

Despite the circumstances, I have fond memories of that first home. In those days, Mom was still pretty lucid, and she knew who we were. We could throw and catch a ball with her, or play swingball (totem tennis) in the garden together. It was important that the time we spent with Mom was purposeful, that we stimulated her and interacted with her in a meaningful way, exercising her brain and cognitive skills. Other times we would sit inside and listen to music. She also loved to paint, so we bought supplies for this, which was therapeutic for her.

While there wasn't really an adjustment period for Mom, there was for the rest of us. But after a couple of months, Mom's home started feeling like an extension of our family home. No matter how old I am or where I live, nothing ever quite has the same feel as 'home'. So although Mom shared her new home with other dementia patients and the homemakers, when I visited, I treated it like I would our old home. I would go into the kitchen and help myself to tea, take anything from the fridge that Mom wanted to eat, and use the various rooms and facilities – while, of course, always being considerate to the other people living there, whose home it was too.

Mom's friends came to visit her as well, not all the time but definitely more so than in the years to come. Sheli in particular would come and spend time with Mom, taking her to the local shops where she could get her Freezochino.

Mom seemed content there, which made coming and going easier on us. Above all, the home provided our family with peace of mind, knowing Mom was being well looked after. Even if something was to happen overnight, there would be carers there who would manage the situation and let us know straightaway.

I knew that she couldn't live forever like that, and the cruelty of the disease played on my mind a lot. I also felt guilty that Mom's life had been reduced to this, even though it wasn't my fault. But if you look hard enough for a silver lining in challenging situations, you can always find one, and back then it was sitting with Mom and learning how to appreciate silence, finding that glimmer of light when everything seemed really dark.

We often make the assumption that a person with a disease like Alzheimer's can't do much, if anything. I don't believe we give them enough credit, or we don't try hard enough with them. One certainty from my experience with Mom, and that of friends and others who have been through their own trauma, is that those who suffer just want to be treated normally. We seem to have been conditioned to think that someone with an illness or a disability is different, therefore they are treated as such, but at the end of the day we are all human beings, and no matter the circumstances we should all be treated with respect and dignity.

Chapter 10

THE SECOND HOME

As mentioned in previous chapters, prior to Mom being diagnosed, when she was still living on the North Shore, she loved to go for walks. Back then we lived in a leafy suburban area, and she would meander through the streets for hours. She knew all our neighbours and would chat to people along the way. One day while on a walk, she found a scarf lying on the ground, so she picked it up and took it with her. She was insistent on finding who the scarf belonged to so that she could return it. She persisted in walking for the rest of that day until, finally, she came across an elderly lady who turned out to be the scarf's owner. This lady, a Jewish woman called Sonia who was well known locally, had written several cookbooks, and for years after this encounter she'd drop recipes into Mom's letterbox.

Fast-forward, and Mom had been living in the home in the North Shore for a year or so when a room became available in a place more easily accessible to all of us. Also, the new place was part of a group of homes we had familiarity with, so we were confident that Mom's level of care would be of a good standard. In any event, the move to the second home was relatively seamless.

This new home had a relatively small number of other residents, all of whom had some form of dementia, apart from one lady in her nineties whose mind was as sharp as anything and who lived there simply due to old age. This woman ruled the house: she had been the matriarch of her family and she took that role into the home. She was the kind of person who commanded attention, but in a subtle and respectful way. It turned out this was Mom's scarfed cookbook author. Sonia was shocked to find out that Mom, such a young woman who only a few years earlier looked so well, had been diagnosed with Alzheimer's. Mom was in her late fifties and had minimal brain functionality, and here was a ninety-year-old who was still completely on the ball. Mom should have had her whole life to look forward to, yet every day was a physical and mental challenge for her. Sonia read the newspaper every day, to the point that she knew everything that was going on in the stock market. At any rate, the two of them would now be sharing a home.

By now, Mom had settled into her new life, having pretty much forgotten her former life. She no longer asked about her old home or questioned where she was. But she had regressed a lot during her stay in the first home, her vibrant personality now overshadowed by the relentless deterioration of her brain. She would often have this glazed look on her face, as if she was staring at nothing and into nowhere, but I could see the sadness in her eyes and wondered if a part of her knew what was actually going on. Another personal discomfort was that it wasn't always easy to spend time with Mom. One hour could feel like many when we were just sitting around, not doing anything. I can fully understand why Dad, who'd spend so many hours with Mom each day, needed to keep doing things to pass the time: read the newspaper, help feed Mom her meals, or just sit on the couch with her and watch TV.

The residents in the second home had varying levels of dementia, but were advanced enough that interactions between them were minimal to non-existent. They would sit side by side to watch TV and eat meals, but rarely did they talk or otherwise engage with one another. However, when we visited, we would always interact with the other residents and their families. Knowing that people with Alzheimer's can struggle to construct sentences or otherwise converse, we would find other ways of communicating. I used to love it when a resident would get fixated on a story, one of the handful of things they remembered, and keep retelling it with enthusiasm and pride. One of the ladies would always talk about her pottery hobby and what she had created, repeating herself over and over, but I'd listen like it was the first time I had heard the story. Another resident would continually sing the same song, and I'd appreciate it every time. You learn a new level of patience for people with Alzheimer's, patience you never thought you had.

We took a lot of our old family photo albums to Mom's new home and spent hours going through them with her, just getting lost in them. It was a really comforting activity, because even though Mom's memory had deteriorated, when she looked at the photos, she would often smile as if an image had triggered a memory. Those moments were special.

Dad would still go and visit every day, and most evenings he would stay for dinner too. When Mom had eaten her food, she would rest her head on Dad's shoulder and drift off; she couldn't really talk at this stage and sometimes it was easier for her to just disengage. But Dad and Sonia, who was extremely intelligent and worldly, would chat about everything from politics to economics and life in general, filling the evening with interesting conversation. Dad also struck up a relationship with Sonia's children.

It made his time there more enjoyable, having other people to talk to, and I'm sure it meant a lot to them too.

Every Friday afternoon, one of the residents would get all dressed up and sit in the living room near the front door. Her family would then pick her up and take her back to their home for Shabbat dinner. She was very well dressed and groomed, and you could tell how much this meant to her, to be having dinner with her family. Watching her wait like that was bittersweet for me, prompting me to think about the loneliness that people can feel when they are isolated from their family in such circumstances. It also made me think about how this terrible disease of dementia had torn Mom from us, and separated countless other loved ones.

* * *

Mom loved few things more than feeling the sun on her face. Being outside and in fresh air on a sunny day was good for her. So Dad would always try to take Mom for a little walk outside. One afternoon, just as the sun was starting to set, they went for a stroll down a nearby street. Suddenly, as they were approaching a bus stop, Mom stopped and wouldn't move. Dad realised she had stopped walking because there was a shadow in front of her and Mom perceived it as a hole in the ground. Dad tried to reason with her but she couldn't comprehend that it was just a shadow and refused to walk on, convinced she would fall in. They had to walk around it.

It's impossible to reason with a person whose brain doesn't function in the way that is typically expected. Things that make complete sense to us simply don't compute for someone with Alzheimer's However, in light of what was waiting for us on the horizon, maybe Mom really did see *more* than just a shadow. Perhaps, deep in the shadow, she could see the darkness that lay ahead.

* * *

All the hardships we had gone through by the time Mom moved into that second home meant I naively felt equipped to deal with anything. I had less tolerance for bullshit, but I had also become more respectful towards other people generally. And then something happened that changed me, leaving an invisible scar. Something that almost made me lose sight of the good in people and caused unimaginable trauma. Today, my sadness and disappointment, my anger, my desire to make those responsible understand the pain they caused us, continue to run so deep that I wonder if I will ever heal. But then I remember Mom, so full of grace and kindness, and I know I can rise above this. Kindness doesn't always win, but I think about Mom's legacy and it reminds me of how I want to be remembered and what I stand for. I remind myself that my mission in life is to educate people about Alzheimer's disease and other forms of dementia, so as to ensure that no-one else will have to experience what we did.

It all happened when Mom had been living in her second home for around a year and Dad was still spending most of his time there. This meant he was privy to almost everything that happened at the home. He would also often help out other residents when they needed something. Hand on heart, I can say that he had the purest of intentions in everything he did, but I can see how his feelings of helplessness may have resulted in some of his actions not being understood. It was this dynamic that led to an event that destroyed the stability we had come to experience. It broke our hearts as the people we relied on most and who had initially led us through this confusing new world let us down.

The details are not completely clear, as I only have the accounts of others to go by. But they suggest that Dad, while visiting Mom, overrode an internal process and called an ambulance to assist a resident who had fallen down. Dad, who has always tried to do the right thing, felt the home was not doing enough in waiting for a nurse to arrive to attend to the resident, so he contacted the person's family to obtain their permission to call the ambulance.

The exact interactions that occurred between Dad and the staff at the home are unclear. Accusations of improper behaviour were directed both ways. But one thing that was clear to me at the time was that the resident's family was thankful that Dad had done what he had. Knowing that, I thought that any negative actions could be dealt with in a firm but professional manner, bearing in mind the close relationships that had developed between my family and the people who provided the care Mom was receiving. How wrong I was.

What proceeded to happen was, for my family and me, an unimaginable nightmare. I was not involved in the initial conversations, but the message that came out of them was clear – Mom's contract with the home was to be terminated. There were three people involved in this decision, two of whom were the people we had most trusted to help our family navigate this awful disease, people who had warned us how difficult the dementia journey could be and how it could break families apart. Yet here they were, facilitating a new fracturing of our family. Rather than deal with the issue at hand, they severed our connection, and had Mom removed from the home.

To this day, I can't reconcile what happened. I can't come to terms with how anyone could do this to a family that was suffering so much. In my head, I've reviewed all the meetings my brothers and I had with the decision-makers, but I still can't fully comprehend what happened. I've thought through every scenario imaginable, trying to see it from their perspective – maybe Dad argued about the fees he paid; maybe he expressed his feelings in a way he did not mean; he was never physically aggressive, but maybe he had let his words be – but I still can't see it. As a family we were respectful in the home, spent so much time there, including with all the other residents, for whom Greg's children were a regular source of happiness. I still can't come up with a reason to justify that heartless decision to make Mom leave the home.

In the weeks that followed, Dad strove to find an alternative place for Mom, and finally he did. That whole period was made much more painful by the fact that we no longer felt welcome at the home, and we were caught between the dread of having to be there and the desire to be with Mom. To put it mildly, it was very unpleasant.

I remember, on the final day, sitting on the bed in Mom's room, surrounded by all of her belongings, which we'd packed. Her room was by the front door, so there was no need to go further into the house. As I looked around the bare room, it felt soulless and cold, reflecting exactly how I was feeling. The homemakers came into the room to say goodbye, heartbroken at seeing Mom go. I could feel their loss as much as ours, and saying goodbye to these people who had looked after Mom unconditionally, and to whom I was so grateful, was very sad.

We took Mom's belongings, closed the door and never looked back. But the sadness and pain followed us. It has been with us all these years. It made me question people, showed me an ugly side of humankind. It also confirmed to me that, even in the best aged-care facilities, there is still room for greater compassion and improved processes.

Chapter 11

THE FINAL HOME

When it sunk in that we only had a month to find Mom a new place to live, we went into panic mode. Bringing her home wasn't an option, and we knew from previous experience that vacancies in the places we most liked were scarce. We were privileged in being able to afford a particular type of home, one that didn't feel like a typical old-age home and could give Mom specialised care, but that also meant we put pressure on ourselves to keep looking until we found just the right place. In the case of Mom's third (and what would be her final) home, we had to compromise: we found another home that, while not perfect, worked for a bunch of reasons. For one thing it was nearby, which definitely suited us. It was more of a standard aged-care facility, but it still had high-care options that were suitable for people with Alzheimer's. And while the nurses and carers weren't specifically trained in dementia care, their skills were adequate for Mom, considering the stage she was at.

Over the years, we'd looked at quite a few care facilities. Dad and I saw one home that actually resembled a prison: the building was old and in poor condition; the facilities were basic; the place was unwelcoming – all in all, it felt like somewhere you'd lock people up, not look after people who weren't able to care for themselves. As we were inspecting it, I said to Dad there was no way I would ever put Mom in there. It was appalling to us, but we also knew such places are the reality for many people who cannot afford a better option.

When we walked into Mom's new home for the first time, it was a bit of a shock in comparison to her previous homes. When we'd originally looked at homes for Mom, they were dementia-specific homes, rather than aged-care homes. But this time, we were looking at aged-care homes and all-care type facilities, which was new to us. It wasn't bad by any stretch of the imagination, and if I'm completely honest, it was more that it was difficult for my family to accept that *any* place would be good enough – we always wanted the best for Mom. The new place was actually very clean and well looked after. It had two floors, each housing residents' rooms, a kitchen, a dining area, and a common area for people to spend time in. But the accommodation was reminiscent of hospital rooms, with hospital-like beds and linen, and the building had that classic nursing home smell to it.

This facility was also more confronting because it was permeated by a sense of finality. Typically, such places are a person's last residence before they pass. Because of Mom's age – barely sixty years old – it was hard to come to terms with the fact that she would now be living in this kind of home. The other residents were mostly quite a bit older than Mom and suffered from various conditions: some had dementia, one woman had Parkinson's disease, and another woman had had a fall and needed assisted living. We were pressed for time, though, and no other suitable options had presented themselves. This meant the choice had kind of been made for us.

Aside from the trauma of what had led us to the new home, the move was easy. No doubt Mom felt confused and disoriented by the unfamiliar surroundings, but I don't believe she was overly aware of what was happening. The hardest thing about it was that my brothers, Dad and I had to again familiarise ourselves with a new home, new carers and new processes, and get Mom set up yet again. It was tiring.

Mom had to share a room with another woman as no single rooms were available. I wasn't comfortable with this – I felt like we were letting Mom down – but we had no choice. The two beds were separated by a curtain, much like in a hospital room. The room was on the ground floor, and on Mom's side was a door that opened to an outside area where we could take Mom and sit with her. Mom and the other woman each had a TV opposite their bed, a small wardrobe and a bedside table. It was very basic, and it took some getting used to, but Mom actually didn't need much more than that.

The thing I found hardest at the beginning of Mom's stay was the loss of privacy. No longer could we go into Mom's room, close the door and be alone with her. There was someone else we now had to consider, an older lady who, as the months went by, spent more and more time in bed, and she would also be visited by family members. There was a lot of activity more generally, too, because the home had a lot more residents than we'd become used to in the previous places.

At that time, Mom was still walking unassisted, although it was getting harder for her to get around, and her communication abilities had also further decreased. She was reliant on help for most things. Things we had taken for granted, which Mom had been doing her entire life, were now complex and confusing tasks. For instance, although she could feed herself most of the time, there were still occasions when she resembled a toddler eating, food going everywhere except in her mouth. Initially it was heartbreaking to watch, but after a while I became desensitised to it.

Every morning the staff would help wash and dress the residents, preparing them for the day. Dad was still insistent that Mom was properly dressed and groomed every single day. Sometimes Mom's hair and make-up would be a little overdone – doing hair and make-up admittedly wasn't a specialty of the carers – but the main thing was that Dad's wishes had been followed, and that was important to him. He hated the idea of anyone staying in pyjamas or wearing a tracksuit all day long; even now, Dad's version of casual is a pair of pants and a collared shirt.

The dining room was pretty basic, with a door that led out to a garden. Everyone ate their meals there, except those residents who were bed-bound and had food taken directly to their rooms. I spent a lot of time in the dining room with Mom, as I'd visit after work when it was time for dinner, or around lunchtime on the weekend. During mealtimes, everyone had an allocated place to sit. Mom would sit at a table with five other people, none of whom spoke to anyone – it was sad to see all these people sitting together but essentially alone. By contrast, there was another group of women who would talk throughout their meals. I couldn't really make out what they were talking about, but it reminded me of old friends chatting over food, remembering the good old days. Then there was an old man who mostly sat alone and needed to be fed by someone, and who always struck a chord with me. *Is that what life comes to?* I'd think to myself. *Living in an old-age home, eating meals alone?* It really made me think about getting old and how cruel it can be.

After breakfast, the residents were accompanied back to their rooms, or to the common area or out into the garden, which had tables and chairs where they could sit in the sunshine. We insisted that someone take Mom for a walk or did an activity with her every day. Dad also organised for Mom to have her hair professionally done once a week by a visiting hairdresser. This was an additional service that he had to pay for; similarly, there was an extra cost for bringing people into the home to engage Mom in activities. Luckily, because of the personal and financial sacrifices Dad had made in order to look after his family, we were able to provide her with this.

One of the bigger adjustments from life at the previous home was the quality of the food. The new home had to cater for far more residents – cooking for sixty-odd people three times a day isn't easy, nor is taking all of their different preferences and medical issues into account. Most residents seemed OK with what was being served up, but we found it difficult to accept that this was what Mom would be eating. Dad complained about the food a lot – and it was warranted. The meals were quite basic – meat or chicken and vegetables or pasta – and the taste was pretty average, certainly not exciting. Sometimes, instead of having Mom eat whatever was on the menu, we would just request a sandwich for her, which seemed the better option.

A more contentious issue was that, when Mom had first moved in, we'd explained to the staff that she was kosher and couldn't eat pork, ham or shellfish. So it used to really aggravate me when they'd serve Mom soup that had ham in it, or a meal containing pork. We had to be diligent in maintaining Mom's values and culture. Just because she was no longer able to speak for herself did not mean she should have to give up all the things she believed in and had practised during her life. Again, we had to keep being Mom's voice.

* * *

I'll admit to having mixed feelings about Mom's time in that home, but equally I'll admit that it quickly became a place where we spent a lot of time and made some lasting memories. Among all the sadness, we did have some beautiful moments with Mom. Taking her outside and sitting with her became an important part of our routine. I loved sitting with her in the fresh air, even during winter – when it was cold, I'd take a blanket to cover her. Besides, there always seemed to be a spot of sunshine for us to sit in, and as the sun moved throughout the day, we would follow it.

When the grandchildren came to visit, which was most weekends, they would run straight to their *bobba*. They would all get the chance to push her wheelchair in the garden. The kids learned from an early age to always go and say hello and give Bobba a hug as soon as they saw her. They also knew where the biscuits were and would inevitably have their treat in the sunshine with Mom. The kids seemed to develop a sense of empathy from a young age, a beautiful gift that I see them demonstrating in their lives today.

Dad would keep some soccer balls in his car so that when the kids came to visit, they could spend hours kicking them around a patch of grass, challenging each other to mini soccer matches. That garden became their playground, and their memories of visiting Bobba are filled with hours spent playing in the open air, rather than sitting inside a depressing old-age home. They would even bring their bikes and scooters and go riding around the outside paths, going faster and faster, seeing who could do the fastest lap. On weekends, Dad would always stop off at his favourite produce shop and buy dried mango and other fruit for everyone to enjoy; he loved spoiling the kids and seeing them share treats with Bobba.

It soon got to the stage where it was too difficult to take Mom out on her birthday or on Mother's Day, so we celebrated these occasions, as well as anniversaries and Jewish holidays, at the home – we brought the celebrations to her. We would bring a cake or other sweets, or Dad would pick up fish and chips from a shop down the road. On Kol Nidrei night, Dad and I would go and eat our last meal before the fast with Mom at the home. Even though she wouldn't be fasting with us, it was important to us that she was still a part of our traditions. We missed the food that Mom used to prepare for the occasion – chicken soup, roast meat and vegetables, and a round *challah* – but we'd have to settle for chicken that Dad would pick up from a Kosher place nearby.

When Mom had first moved into that final home, she could still walk and converse with us, but this all changed very quickly. It was almost as if she knew this home would be her final one, and she was now ready to stop fighting and let go of what was left of her independence, and succumb to the disease. Suddenly, she needed assistance to walk, and then walking became too difficult and she was put into a wheelchair. When it first happened, we would wheel Mom where she wanted to go, whether it be the common area, dining room or outside, and the staff would transfer Mom from the wheelchair into a chair. It took two people to do it, as she had put on quite a lot of weight.

Dad insisted this approach for as long as possible, as a proper chair was much more comfortable for her. But after a while it just became too difficult to lift Mom up, and so, after she had showered and dressed in the morning, she would be put into the wheelchair and there she would stay for the rest of the day, until she went to bed. I can only imagine how uncomfortable it was for Mom to sit in that chair all day.

Seeing Mom in a wheelchair was heartbreaking. It took the situation we were dealing with to another level. We could sense she was uncomfortable but there wasn't another option: if we wanted Mom to be mobile, she needed to be in a wheelchair. Soon, however, because Mom's weight continued to balloon, the wheelchair became too small and we needed to get her into something bigger and more comfortable, especially considering she spent most of her waking hours in that chair. So we bought a wider wheelchair, something she could almost lie down in. The problems didn't stop there, though. As Mom was pretty much confined to her wheelchair, she began to develop bed sores, which then had to be treated.

* * *

I don't recall the exact moment when I realised that Mom didn't know who I was anymore. There had been many times over the years when she'd been confused about our identities, interspersed with moments of lucidity when she would remember our names. But at some point while staying in that home, she well and truly forgot who we were. Dad had a really hard time coming to terms with that. He persisted in holding her hand whenever he was with her, insisting the rest of us do the same, clinging to the idea that even if she couldn't acknowledge us directly, she would always know who we were deep down. Part of me believed that too, or at least wanted to believe it, but for the most part I accepted what had happened. I'd been told right at the start, when Mom was first diagnosed, that her condition would get to a point where she wouldn't recognise us anymore, where she wouldn't remember who we were. I'd always known that day was coming, and I'd been prepared for it. I did hold onto Mom's hand, but it was more to reinforce to me that we were still in each other's presence, holding time and space for each other, which was all we really had.

With this lack of recognition, I felt the last remaining light in Mom had gone out. But it didn't really change anything: she was always going to be my mom, and I was always going to be her daughter.

* * *

In some ways, out of the different homes that Mom stayed in, the last one felt most like it was *her* home. Perhaps it was because we all knew this would be her last. We couldn't foresee her going anywhere else, and the staff there were going to provide the necessary care right up until the end, including palliative care if needed. Another reason was that, when our family was there, we would almost take over the place, especially the garden. In terms of visitors, Mom definitely received more than anyone else, most probably because of her age and the fact that so many of her family and friends lived close by. Mom would have a visitor or multiple visitors most days, particularly on the weekend. In fact, I don't think a day went by without someone coming to see her.

Ryan, the son of my cousin Michael and his wife Jody, had an especially strong bond with Mom. When Ryan was around seven years old, Jody would bring him to visit Mom every few weeks, and you could tell he absolutely loved it. It was the most heartwarming thing to witness. I don't know what it was, but Ryan had this beautiful love for Mom, and every time he was there, Mom would have a big smile on her face. I don't think any of us will ever fully understand the authentic connection between Mom and Ryan. They held something unique, a connection that was just between them, and only they understood how profound it was.

Another joyful memory involves the common room. We had been told that Mom would respond well to sensory items, and as luck would have it, the staff had filled the common room with all types of sensory stimulation for the residents. The walls were cluttered with fluffy balls and other types of soft toys. Eventually we got Mom an apron that had different sensory items on it. She wore that apron every day, occupying herself by playing with the various things on it. More than just part of her daily uniform, it became like a safety blanket and provided her with much comfort.

Something that was really drummed into me during this time was that old-age homes are extremely transient places, with residents continually coming and going. I did come across people who had been in the home for many years, but some were only there for a short time. It was not uncommon to walk into the home and hear that someone had passed away. Either way, it was an opportunity to learn a lot about what other people were experiencing. I found comfort in talking to other family members who had come to visit their loved ones, as we were all going through something similar.

Mom had been at the home for a while when a family we already knew arrived to settle their husband/father into the home. Cancer had taken almost complete control of his body, but his mind was unaffected for the most part. One day while visiting Mom, I bumped into the man's wife, who was sitting outside his room, and stopped to have a chat. The cancer was advancing quickly: the timeframe was more months than years. The man was completely sound of mind and knew exactly what was going on, but his body had completely failed him; he was unable to even get out of bed. Mom, on the other hand, had some physical control but absolutely no idea what was going on, as her mind had failed her long ago.

The man's wife and I talked about whether it was worse to be afflicted in your mind and be unaware of what was happening to you, or your body and be unable to perform physical tasks. I found myself taking comfort in the belief that it would be worse to have a functioning mind, to be aware of your situation, but powerless to change it. When it came to my mother, there was no way to know what she was thinking or feeling, but my hope was that she had become blissfully unaware, and that time had no consequence for her.

Another resident by the name of Reggie ended up having quite the relationship with Mom. She would have been in her eighties, and she'd had a bad fall a few years earlier that, with her husband having passed away, had left her unable to look after herself. Reggie was like the man with cancer: sound of mind, but her body had let her down. She had to use a walker to slowly get around and often preferred spending hours in her bedroom watching

TV, being more comfortable lying down. Of course, this meant she felt very isolated, more so because her family visited only infrequently. But Reggie began gravitating to Mom, and in turn we did to her. One trait we really took to was her sense of humour. Just like my father and me, she would laugh at the most obscure things, and she and Dad would tell each other stories and laugh at things most other people wouldn't find the slightest bit funny.

From the day we met Reggie, she was always eager to chat and let us know everything that was happening around the home: she had eyes and ears everywhere. Reggie took a real liking to Mom, and over time she became my mother's keeper, sitting with Mom, talking to her and watching over her. When Mom was no longer able to walk, the nurses would wheel her into Reggie's room so the two of them could keep each other company. Reggie was 40 per cent deaf and 60 per cent blind as a result of her fall, and Mom's senses weren't too flash either, so the two of them would sit in Reggie's room with the TV blaring, but it never bothered either of them. The circumstances gave Reggie a sense of purpose, and at the same time reassured us that Mom was never entirely alone. We found it immensely comforting to know that when we left the home, Reggie would be there for Mom, and vice versa.

One time Reggie caught some kind of virus and Dad decided he didn't want Mom sitting in her room, in case she was also infected. That was hard for us, knowing Mom would be alone, and it was certainly just as hard for Reggie. There was an upside in that, before Reggie fell ill, the staff had been tending towards leaving Mom in Reggie's room all day rather than taking her outside for her daily dose of sunshine and fresh air, but now they were taking Mom out again. Still, the pair had become practically inseparable, so keeping them apart wasn't great. Fortunately, Reggie soon recovered and Mom found her way back into her friend's room – and the carers took Mom's need for time outside much more seriously from then on, too.

Reggie also became a confidant to my father. If something was wrong, Dad would often tell her all about it. I'm not sure if he told her things because she was a good listener or because he thought she could be trusted not to divulge anything to anyone else, or both. Regardless, Reggie would always share with me what Dad had told her when I came to visit. This wasn't out of duplicity. It was because she cared about us all and wanted us to know what was going on with each other.

Reggie didn't love the food in the home either. So when Dad brought Mom chocolates, which he loved feeding to her, he also supplied them to Reggie. She always had a stash in the drawer next to her bed, to which I occasionally contributed, especially at Easter or Christmas. Reggie savoured the chocolate and most days she slowly chipped away at it.

* * *

At times it felt like Mom's battle with Alzheimer's would go on forever, that there was no timeline. But while it could be all-consuming, the rest of life had to go on. I was building a career, having started my own business, and work was important to me. When I was at work, I felt more or less in control, which was something I craved after spending time with Mom. I tried to stay social, too, and hang out with my friends when I could. And then there were times, after a long day of work, when I just wanted to go straight home and be alone, when I simply didn't have it in me to visit. I don't regret that. While I had to sustain Mom, I knew I had to sustain myself as well.

One thing I did religiously was visit Mom every Saturday and Sunday. It became part of my weekend routine, and I looked forward to the afternoons we would spend together, and with the rest of the family. It was actually a time when Greg, Ricky and I could reconnect. Over the years we'd split our time with Mom so she was alone as little as possible, which meant we rarely had quality time together as siblings. Now we were spending much more time together as a family. I also think those afternoons with Mom at the home enabled me to take a break from everything else in my life, to simply stop and breathe, cosy in my family's little shared bubble. I enjoyed the stillness of not doing anything, of not needing to rush, or to be anywhere else.

Despite how fulfilling it could be, there were times when I wanted to be anywhere – on a beach, in a forest, out socialising – other than in an old-age home. An intense feeling would wash over me that Mom and Dad shouldn't be there either, in that nursing home. Mixed emotions struck me all the time. Knowing how to feel was impossible. If I was happy, I felt guilty. If I was sad, I was angry about being sad. Sometimes it was easier not to feel at all. And that's often what I did. I'd become numb to it all.

* * *

By the beginning of 2019, Mom was completely wheelchair-bound and spent most of each day just sitting there, passing time. Her ability to interact with anyone was pretty much gone. You could say that Mom's condition had somewhat stabilised in that home, that she'd already suffered so much deprivation that there simply wasn't that much more she could lose. Her quality of life was terrible. It was as though she was merely existing rather than living.

In April of that year, the home called Dad to say that Mom had taken a turn for the worse and they didn't think she had more than a week to live. Panicked by this news, my heart beat faster, my mind went into overdrive, and I felt transported to the moment of finality – the moment Mom would pass away. I wanted to rush over there and be with Mom, not knowing how much time was left. When I finally stopped to take a breath, a sense of familiarity took over. We had been here before, getting bad news in a phone call; this might just be the past repeating itself. Then another emotion swept over me and everything felt foreign again, as if this was the very first time I had received news like this.

When I finally arrived at the home, I found Mom lying in her bed with a glazed look, unresponsive, seemingly lifeless. She was physically there but in every other way she was absent. In the months leading up to this, she had been having issues swallowing and would mostly eat liquid or soft foods. But now she had stopped eating entirely and was barely drinking fluids. I spent the next few days by her side. I'd arrive in the morning with my laptop, sit next to her and do work – because I worked for myself, I had the luxury of working from anywhere. Dad, my brothers and Mom's brothers came in and out during the day, also sitting with her or just waiting. Her condition didn't seem to get worse, but there were moments when I felt like it was the beginning of the end, when she looked even more pale and sickly, expressionless, with a profound sense of sadness about her.

A week passed ... and suddenly she snapped out of it and started eating again. Mom started to seem more like her old self again, or closer to how she had once been anyway. We had experienced so many fluctuations and ups and downs that it was hard to remember how Mom was before she began to decline.

What a mind-fuck! In the course of that week, I'd prepared myself for losing her. It meant that, when Mom recovered, I was incredibly relieved but also really agitated and angry for having to go through all those emotions, getting ready for the final goodbye and contemplating what life would be like afterwards. It was a week during which I had put everything else on hold, existing only within the walls of the home, focused on making sure the person I loved was not alone, not wanting to have any regrets. It's an emotional roller-coaster that no-one can prepare you for.

After this new close call, we were advised by a doctor to establish an end-of-life plan for Mom, because she didn't have much time left – she was nearing the last few stages of Alzheimer's that would inevitably lead to her passing. These are some of the toughest decisions you will ever have to make for someone else. You have to decide what happens to someone when their mortality is in the balance: when to prolong their life, and when to say goodbye. As a family, we had to decide whether or not to resuscitate Mom if it came to that. It seemed such an unfair decision, but one we had to make, taking into account not only what was best for Mom but what was best for us too.

Naturally, you want to prolong someone's life. You want to give them every chance to live as long as possible. But Mom wasn't living. This wasn't a way of life. And so finally, as a family, we made the decision that should she suffer a major medical event, we would opt for 'Do not resuscitate'. It was an awful thing to contemplate, but in fact it turned out to be a pretty simple choice. We consulted with the doctor, and each other, and unanimously made the decision. It was too hard seeing Mom struggle through life every day, her dignity compromised by Alzheimer's. We were sure it was not a life she would have wanted to prolong, and it felt selfish of us to do so knowing that she had fought long and hard to be the best she could be over the course of her life, in the toughest times and under the worst conditions.

As we deliberated, little did we know that six months later, we would receive our last call from the home.

Chapter 12

THE FUNERAL

Throughout Mom's illness, I kept getting told how little time she had left, so I ended up saying goodbye every day for eight years. Every time another little piece of her drifted away, I said goodbye to it. A sense of loss came with every regression, and with each loss came a period of mourning. So when Mom did finally pass, it was a moment I had spent almost a decade anticipating and readying myself for.

In the Jewish religion, it is customary to bury the deceased as soon as possible. In Mom's case, because she passed away on the Jewish holiday of Yom Kippur, we were unable to do anything for almost twenty-four hours. Finally, my dad, my brothers and I went to the Chevra Kadisha, which was situated in an old building that was strangely reminiscent of an old-age home, with lots of dark wood and creaky doors and floors – the kind of place that can make a low mood even lower. We sat around a large table and went through all the logistics.

It was a surreal time. Among all the pain and sadness, we needed to organise a funeral and have a death certificate prepared. On the one hand, we were dealing with Mom's loss and all the emotions that came with it, and on the other hand, we needed to be practical and get her affairs in order.

Jewish funerals are all standard, without frills or extravagance. Because they are so understated, it makes the situation easier to bear, and the arrangements easy to make. You don't even have to choose a casket. Once we had finalised the details, we left the Chevra Kadisha and walked across the road to a café. That was strange too, organising the details of a funeral one minute and sipping a cup of coffee the next – perhaps a stark reminder amidst the devastation that life must go on. Mom certainly wouldn't have wanted it any other way. She would've been satisfied by her husband and kids remembering her, but not fussing over her.

That evening, we sat down with the rabbi to talk about Mom. Our rabbi didn't know my mom well, as he was fairly new and Mom was already very sick by the time he joined the synagogue. However, he had a remarkable ability to be completely present and hold on to every word we spoke. Rabbi Dovi listened intently as we reflected on who Mom had been in her early years – what kind of mother, wife, sister and friend we all recalled. It was a comfort during the saddest of times, reminiscing about someone we loved, someone who had such a significant impact on each of our lives. It allowed us to remember the loving, caring and kind person she was, the dedicated mother, the fun-loving friend. So often when you are faced with adversity, it's hard to find the light. Sharing those fond memories of Mom and speaking so proudly about who she was brightened my soul.

In preparation for the funeral, Mom's body was bathed and cleansed, and then she was dressed for burial in the same kind of white cloth that every deceased Jewish person is dressed in. This custom is one of the most profound I have ever experienced. Everyone is born into the world the same: naked. And when we die, we leave the world similarly naked. It is irrelevant how much money you made, what car you drove, how big your house was or what you did for work. Birth and death are the only two commonalities between all people. That is why there is no need to bury the deceased in flashy clothes or with any possessions. This simple approach brings everyone back down to earth, as it were, and reminds us all what really matters in this world: our shared humanity.

The Long Goodbye

I remember panicking before the funeral because I did not have a long black skirt or other appropriate clothing to wear. Long black skirts are not a common item in my wardrobe, and I am not a regular synagogue-goer. In fact, I am the only one in the family who doesn't really attend. So my best friend, Moss, the sister I never had, who knows me better than anyone, ran around a shopping centre picking out dress and shoe options for me. When I'd chosen what I wanted, she returned the rest. It was such a simple thing, but it was so seriously helpful, giving me one less thing to think about.

Waking up on the morning of the funeral involved not so much panic as a sense of strangeness, one of those days when you have to think twice about what you're supposed to be doing that day. I had thought about this day many times. I'd contemplated how I would feel, or how I was supposed to feel. I'd reflected on who would be there, and how I would feel about some of them, in particular the ones I felt anger towards. It's easy to show up at the end of someone's life to pay your respects. The people who really stood out to me were the ones who'd shown up throughout those eight years – through both the good times and the really tough times.

It was spring but I remember that morning being chilly. I got dressed, did my hair and drove to Greg's house, then

Dad drove us to the cemetery from there, a trip of about half an hour. The car ride was mostly silent, and Dad was teary. As we approached the Ohel (a structure built around a Jewish grave as a sign of the prominence of the deceased), things started to become more real. Before a Jewish funeral, the immediate family of the deceased waits around the back of the Ohel and only enters when the body is brought in, and generally, close family members will come and greet you there while everyone else takes a seat inside. I remember standing there feeling annoyed that people were coming up to us. I just wanted a moment with my immediate family. Also, I hate being the centre of attention; it makes me feel uncomfortable, and I prefer to fly under the radar. But there was nothing I could do because Mom's funeral was a big thing – my uncle and aunt from Perth came, my cousin from Melbourne flew in, and other friends and family made a huge effort to be there. In Jewish law, attending a funeral and burial is considered a 'religious obligation'. Your presence is the most important thing you can contribute.

Rabbi Dovi arrived and again talked us through the proceedings, then it was time to enter the Ohel. Walking in, I was greeted by a sea of faces – family and friends, new and old. Not surprisingly, the mood was sombre, not only due to the loss of Mom, but because many of those present had relatives, spouses and friends buried at that particular cemetery. Also, in Jewish culture, we don't celebrate a life in the way you would at a secular funeral or wake; rather, the act of remembering means beginning the mourning process.

My brothers, father and I sat in the first row, directly in front of the coffin. Rabbi Dovi then began speaking about Mom, perfectly capturing her life and legacy. There was some comfort in knowing that, because of where we were seated, no-one could see our faces. Burying a parent, or any loved one for that matter, is obviously a vulnerable time. You feel completely stripped, as if everyone can see deep inside you, even straight through you. I was sure that, at some point, I would start feeling something. But I felt nothing; I was completely numb. I remember saying to myself, *You should be crying, it's weird that you are not crying*, and trying to bring tears to my eyes. But I was dry as a bone. That's the funny thing about expectations. That's all they are – expectations. At the most definitive moment of my mom's passing, I couldn't feel anything except this pure numbness.

I realise now, of course, that numbness *is* a feeling in and of itself. It was a manifestation of my overwhelming relief – not for myself but for Mom, that she no longer had to live with Alzheimer's and a quality of life far less than she deserved.

Throughout the ceremony I held on to Dad, who was crying. It broke my heart to see it. Maybe it's because many of us are conditioned to believe that fathers are the strong ones, the ones who don't show any emotion. Yet I saw Dad get emotional many times over the years when Mom was unwell, longing for the days when she was OK, when they went about their life as normal.

After the ceremony, we all walked behind the coffin down to the gravesite. In Jewish tradition, the immediate family does not participate in the pallbearing. Extended family and close friends are instead called upon. It is customary for six pallbearers to carry the coffin at any one time, swapping with others on the slow journey to the gravesite. We arrived to find the hole already dug, and listened as Jewish prayers were recited, including the Kaddish – the mourner's prayer.

When they started to lower the coffin, I felt a lump form in my throat. If there was ever a moment of finality, this was it. It wasn't a dream. It was reality. I was burying Mom, and it was the final goodbye. It was time for her *neshama* to be released and for Mom to find peace; I don't know if I believe in an afterlife, but I do believe Mom's *neshama* passed into a new life, and that she was reunited with her parents. And yet all I felt inside at that moment was an emptiness.

It is customary for the family of the deceased to throw three shovelfuls of sand into the grave, which makes one of the most horrific sounds I have ever heard, and is always met with wailing. This time, when the first shovelful of sand hit Mom's coffin, I shed my first tear.

* * *

Following the funeral, the culmination of eight years of mixed and harrowing emotions, I found myself leaning into Jewish customs. As someone who is more traditional than religious, I never expected faith in my religion and the practices that had given Mom's dignity back to her to be such a strong anchor in these moments.

It is a Jewish custom to say, 'I wish you a long life,' when you greet a mourner at a funeral, which reflects our culture's emphasis on preserving and saving life. This custom helps people to know what to say at the service, as well as on the Yahrzeit (the anniversary of the death of a parent or loved one) each year. When it's hard to find words of comfort, such customs provide universal certainty and solace.

After the coffin had been lowered, I felt drained and just wanted to leave, but I knew we all had to wait around so everyone could wish us 'a long life'. I've been on the other side of this and know how important it is for a person attending a funeral to have the opportunity to do this. So as much as I wanted to just get in the car and go, I couldn't. Instead, I looked around at everyone who was there and realised how lucky we were to have so many people in our lives who had known Mom, if not personally then through us. Still, the funeral had sucked the energy out of me, and I felt like a robot repeating the same words over and over.

After the funeral, Shiva (the seven days of mourning) – the time of bereavement for Mom's immediate family – began. During Shiva, it is customary to sit on low benches. You remove the cushions from any couches, cover all mirrors, and don't watch TV or listen to music; you don't cut your hair, nor do men shave. You simply mourn the person you have lost. It is a time to reflect, a period devoted to spiritual and emotional health.

I never truly understood the significance of the mourning process until I went through it. Because of the timing of Mom's death, our Shiva was cut short by the Sabbath and a Jewish holiday, but even so, those were some of the most meaningful days I had after losing her. I found that Shiva allows you to sit with your sadness and take all the time you need to acknowledge that something significant has occurred, and that an immediate return to normal life is not necessary. It made me stop and appreciate life, and gave me time to spend with Dad and my brothers in reflection.

Directly after the funeral, we went back to Greg's house. My uncles and cousins and some family friends joined us there, and they all brought food, especially bagels, a traditional Jewish food that symbolises the circle of life.

The Long Goodbye

I just wanted to go home and disappear from the world, but being around people was good for me. What I at first dreaded turned out to be a rare opportunity to sit with family and friends and reminisce about Mom.

We had a notebook and everyone wrote down a story about Mom. I love reading the memories in that book, in particular the one from Mom's cousin Leon. They grew up together, and from all accounts got up to much mischief.

Being the youngest boy of the Jankelowitz clan, I was always put with the young girls at family gatherings. This gave me the privilege of getting to know darling Terry and getting very close to her. We both developed a love of smoking, which in those days was fashionable. So while our parents were playing cards, we were secretly digging in handbags and stealing smokes. We would often lock ourselves in the bathroom pretending only one person was inside and smoke our lungs out. I recall the Wingwam days lying in the long grass near the horses' stables blowing smoke rings into the sky. Terry introduced me to Margot [Leon's wife, a lifelong friend of Mom's], which was a blessing.

A true friend and loving cousin is all I can say about her. Always up to some fun and laughter. We would lie around chatting for hours, music blaring and always on the look out for Ray and Harold [Mom's brothers], who would have dobbed on us to our parents. Terry is one of the most beautiful girls that I was lucky enough to have spent my childhood with. I will miss you forever. Rest in peace my darling.

    Love Leon J

The funeral was held on a Friday morning, which meant we couldn't have prayers that night as it was Shabbat, so we held prayers on the Saturday evening. It is common at these prayers for family members to speak. Public speaking is not my forte, so I left this up to my brothers and Dad. Hearing them speak about Mom was a mixture of a punch to the stomach and a really comfortable, settling feeling. Ricky and Greg were able to articulate Dad's love and devotion to Mom in a way that made so much sense, and it would've put things into perspective for a lot of people. When Dad spoke, I lost it; I couldn't hold back any longer. There's something about seeing Dad sad or hearing him talk about Mom that gets me every time.

Chapter 13

EULOGY
by Ricky Kitay

Our family has been on a journey for the past eight years, but the end came quickly and it was peaceful. Tonight, very briefly I want to give you a snippet of the life of our mother Terry and the journey we have been on as her children over her life.

Our mother's life was so much more than her battle with Alzheimer's, but as this battle has consumed us so intimately, it is unfortunately hard to clearly remember what life was like before.

We do remember and will never forget, as was beautifully articulated by Rabbi Dovi, our mother's warmth, her softness and kindness, her smile and unwavering support for family. She was selfless and refused to be a burden to others even when she should have. I take great comfort in knowing from the numerous messages from friends and family that there are many people who loved our mother and so many people who came into our lives during this period who wished they knew her better. I feel immense pride in listening to the heartfelt anecdotes recalled about our mother, which were both unanimous and consistent in their messages. She was a special human being and an Eshet Chayil in every sense of the word.

But unfortunately, as it is with life and the cards you are dealt, our mom was diagnosed with early-onset Alzheimer's in 2011 at the age of fifty-five. She was cared for at home by my dad for three years with the help of Sheli. She was then cared for by others in care facilities for five years. she moved into the first care facility on 19 October 2014 and passed away on 8 October 2019, corresponding to 10 Tishrei 5779.

The dementia experience is one that does not discriminate and has had a profound impact on the lives of so many. Her closest family members watched as she slowly dissipated from the person she was and who we remember to some morph of her old self. I often asked, 'Who is this person? Who has my mother become, because this isn't who my mother is and who I remember her being?'

I lived at home with Mom and Dad for the first two-and-a-half years of her illness. I had at times an unfortunate but also fortunate viewing of the challenges Mom faced. For example, whether it was the routine of writing out her next day's schedule at night and going over it with her, or whether it was picking out her clothes or cleaning up after her – the strain and pressure we all felt was immense.

Dad felt the brunt of this strain and he was Mom's primary carer. Dad was demanding of others and expected the world, but this came from a place of immense love for our mom and pressure to keep Mom's life as normal and effortless as possible. This was daily, if not hourly, trauma that Dad endured as he watched Mom slip away from him and all of us.

Right from the beginning, up until the end, Dad's sole focus and concern was that his wife Terry was looked after to the highest standard and that she would not be forgotten. Not forgotten by him, his kids, her brothers, sisters-in-law and friends. The highest honour I can pay my father is that he maintained our mother's dignity and love right until the end.

We were all accepting of this disease early on, but Mom said to me she didn't think that this would be the life she would be living. We watched as our mom's face changed. Not physically, but emotionally, as the toll of the disease ran its course.

I vividly remember speaking to Dad shortly before I got married at the end of 2013. He told me how hard it was at home, not because I had moved out, but because the mom he was living with was not the wife he had married. He said to me, 'Mom is different, and however hard it is for us, it's ten times worse for Mom. She knows she is not who she was and is living in this trapped life.'

By late 2014, Mom was in a care facility. I recall my sister-in-law pointing out to us how Mom was looking relaxed, like a weight had been lifted off her shoulders. In her new home, she was the boss, this was her world, her home, her place, and we were the visitors. But as with this disease, you could see the deterioration intimately.

During a series of visits at the end of 2014, I captured these accounts which I'd like to share with you. On 25 November 2014, Mom would sit and paint and only needed a little help with changing the paint colours. 30 November 2014: now Mom needed help to change the paint colours. 2 December 2014: now Mom needed help to paint the picture. And then on 7 December 2014: Mom didn't know what to do with the paintbrush when I put it in her hand. She started to cry and said, 'I don't know what I am doing, help me.'

I often questioned what kind of life this was for Mom. Over the next few years her ability to do so many things was taken away from her. For the last three years, Mom had been confined to either a wheelchair or her bed, not able to walk or verbally communicate. But even through this chaining of her independence, as Mom once called it, her family never wavered.

The Long Goodbye

Dad went to visit Mom daily, and sometimes more than once a day. He spent hours with Mom, and even though she couldn't talk to him, she would squeeze his hand or give him a cheeky smile, knowing he was someone special. Dad spent eight of these years dedicated and devoted to Mom, the years he should have been enjoying life with Mom, looking after their grandchildren and sharing in new experiences together. Her brothers in Australia and sisters-in-law visited weekly without fail. We also have extended family and friends who were very good to Mom and visited her right through to the end.

Looking back, there is so much I am grateful for. As a family, we were lucky to have carers and residents who loved our mother, who looked after her, cared greatly for her and who are also feeling a sense of loss. My daughter, Ali, and nephews Aaron, Dov and Jacob have been introduced to a world of elderly and sick people and have showed compassion and love at such a young age.

As trying as the last eight years have been, we take pride in our memories of who Mom was as a person, and the legacies she left with us. The legacies of Judaism, family, kindness, and those qualities of an Eshet Chayil, have never been clearer when I look back on our journey as a family.

Two things in particular: Mom always impressed upon us the importance of family, and she taught us that life is best faced with a smile and always with consideration for others.

Nothing was ever too much for her. Particularly over the last eight years, she would have been especially proud of how we have strengthened immensely as a family. She would have been proud to know that we have approached our journey with the same attitude, and will continue to face life with this attitude in her memory.

Chapter 14

MISHPACHA (Family)

Dad often talks about the life that he and Mom would have had if Alzheimer's had not come along. His eyes light up when he speaks about how Mom would have spent her days looking after her grandchildren: 'She would have been the best *bobba*.' And she would have. She would have loved her grandchildren unconditionally, doted over them and had all the time in the world for them. The loss Dad feels every day about the later life they could have lived together is by far the saddest part of what happened. For me and my brothers, losing our mother is horrific, but for Dad, losing the person he chose to devote his life to, his wife, whom he would've sacrificed everything for, seems like the ultimate heartache.

When Dad speaks about the retirement he worked so hard for, the time that he and Mom were to enjoy – travelling and being with family – it fills me with sadness. I can vividly picture how it would've unfolded, and the fact that both Mom and Dad have been robbed of this dream is truly soul-crushing.

I've already described how Mom and Dad did everything together. But truthfully, it was more that Dad didn't want to be without Mom. He had this old-fashioned idea that a married couple should want to do everything together, and so they did. Dad isn't the type of guy you'd find having beers at a pub with mates or spending Sunday on the golf course. My parents' weekends were always spent together: lunches with friends, time with family, going to the beach together. Dad would make Mom go with him to Bunnings, a plant nursery or wherever else was on the agenda. He would potter around the garden while Mom would sit on the patio basking in the sun, or prepare lunch inside for everyone.

When Mom was diagnosed with Alzheimer's, Dad was driven by one thing: concern for her wellbeing. He was hell-bent on ensuring her life would stay as normal as possible for as long as possible, and in particular that no-one forgot about her. He was determined that Mom would be at the centre of everything we did, and that she would be cared for to the highest standards. His expectations of others, be it close family, friends or carers, were also very high, as I've described in earlier chapters. Dad would go to any lengths to maintain Mom's dignity and ensure she was treated with the utmost respect. In his eyes, she wasn't to be treated any differently just because she had Alzheimer's – if anything, she was to be treated better. He was not wrong.

When we began the process of investigating what was happening to Mom, Dad was always there. He managed her case, dealing with doctors and other experts, and keeping everyone focused on Mom's care. Too often, people overlooked Mom because of her Alzheimer's. As a result, Dad ensured that everyone, no matter who they were or the role they played in Mom's life, knew that they were dealing with a sensitive human being. Dad was adamant that for as long as possible, Mom would have the final say about things that mattered to her.

This was vital during the diagnosis and initial treatment process, when Dad and Mom were dealing with the doctor from St Vincent's Hospital who was managing Mom's case, including prescribing medication. He was brilliant, and highly regarded in this field, but he lacked a bedside manner. Mom became distraught every time they went to see him. The doctor would perform tests on Mom every month to track what stage of the disease she was in, and these were very confronting for her. She developed great anxiety around going to see him, getting very worked up and teary, knowing he would test her memory and she would in all likelihood fail. I can understand how all this becomes routine for someone who has seen hundreds of patients, but for Mom it was a scary experience.

For the first three years, while Dad was Mom's primary carer at home, things were intense. He was playing multiple roles: husband, carer, taking on all of the household responsibilities that had always been Mom's domain and which Dad had had little or nothing to do with. On top of that, Dad was still going to work every day at his dental practice, earning money so as to provide for Mom and the rest of our family. Under this heavy domestic and professional workload, Dad became resourceful. Everyone at his disposal began playing a significant role in Mom's life as he assigned them roles – from our aunt Sheli, who became a hugely important carer during those first few years at home, to Caz, the nurse who had worked for Dad since his practice opened, and who would bulk-shop for our family at Costco. Caz would also drive all the way to our home to spend time with Mom and undertake activities with her, which Dad would build on by arranging various services from Jewish Care. He made sure that, as much as possible, Mom was not alone while we were all at work.

Everything needed to be scheduled in advance: what Mom would be doing on a particular day, what clothes she would be wearing, what the fridge needed to be stocked with to provide for her breakfast. Dad would also call everyone – and I do mean *everyone* – to ensure they had all committed to a particular time to visit Mom. He would ask them, 'Have you seen her this week? Why did you not visit her today?' One of his goals was to make sure that Mom's visitors were spread out across different days and times, both so she was never alone and to prevent her from being overwhelmed by having a lot of people suddenly arrive to see her. The more people that surrounded Mom, the harder it was for her. This was not just because she struggled to follow conversations but also because, generally speaking, other people would end up talking more to one another rather than engaging with her.

I admitted earlier in this book that there were days when it all felt too much and I wanted a break from it, when I wanted to be free of the responsibility of visiting Mom for just a moment. Dad didn't have those days, or if he did, he pushed through them. For instance, I cannot recall a single day during those five years when Mom was living in care facilities that Dad didn't visit, other than when he was away from Sydney. It was a singular effort that many others struggled to match. Dad witnessed first-hand how Mom's friends slowly started disengaging, even to the point that he would take Mom to the local shops for lunch and friends of hers would purposefully avoid them. It was heartbreaking. These friends were not acting out of spite or malice, only out of discomfort, uncertain of how to engage with Mom. But it was no excuse. The only person this should have been scary for was Mom.

Caring for someone in Mom's condition was so taxing, and once Mom had been moved into a home, it would've been perfectly understandable if Dad had left the caring up to the staff. But he remained 100 per cent on top of her needs. During every visit, he would check she had been properly bathed, that her clothes were clean, her hair had been washed and dried, she had make-up on and her teeth had been brushed. He would make sure that her days were populated with activities, such as a walk around the block or having her wheelchair pushed around the garden, even if that meant bringing in extra resources. He would also do things like leave chocolates next to Mom's bed and bring other treats for her.

Without needing to announce it, Dad was Mom's advocate right from the beginning. The role came naturally. Dad noticed everything, constantly picking up on things that weren't up to scratch in the homes Mom lived in, from the quality of the food to the activities being offered – or the lack thereof. Overall, Mom's carers did a wonderful job, but on occasion Dad would find she had just been sitting in her room for a lengthy period, and he would demand she be given some stimulation.

On a few occasions, Mom's last home decreed that no visitors were allowed due to an outbreak of flu. Dad refused to classify himself as a visitor – he was Terry's husband, and nothing was going to keep him from seeing his wife. He would put on a mask and march straight through the front door, and no-one dared stop him.

Dad's attitude to care extended beyond Mom to the other residents. If someone wasn't able to feed themselves and all the staff were otherwise occupied, Dad would assist. If he saw another resident in need or distress, he would help. If he saw something he was unhappy about, the care facility would know about it and he wouldn't stop complaining until something was done about it.

Dad put his life on hold while Mom was ill; he devoted all his time outside of work to taking care of her. Even after she'd passed, he still wanted the very best for her, including choosing her gravestone, which was something he did with so much consideration. First, he ensured that the choice wasn't ostentatious and that it reflected who Mom was. Even though Mom wasn't physically there, it was important to him that her gravestone be what she would have wanted. He pays to have the gravestone cleaned regularly and when he goes to visit, he always takes a cloth to keep it tidy. To this day, his love for Mom remains strong.

Mom may be gone, but she will never forgotten. One thing Alzheimer's could never take from her was her *neshama* (soul). So much of her *neshama* shone through her. Whenever she smiled, we were reminded for a moment of who Mom really was.

To this day, I will be forever grateful for the sacrifices Dad made for Mom. Amid all the sadness, devastation and complications that we faced as a family, Dad's unequivocal love and devotion to Mom and how he cared for her was by far the thing that stood out to me the most.

* * *

Growing up, I was the sister between two brothers. Some might say the typical middle child and only girl, but I consider my middle-child syndrome as something of a blessing. My brothers were very sporty, which meant I was the wicketkeeper, goalkeeper and any other position in the sporting team that was needed. My brothers would also help me practise netball and play tennis with me. Throughout life, they were never overly protective, which suited me as I was somewhat always on my own path. Being in the middle, I was closer in age to both Greg and Ricky than they were to each other, and in our teens and early twenties, our lives and friends were interconnected and we spent a lot of time together. During uni days, Ricky and I would spend many afternoons and nights watching movies together.

As we have grown older, my brothers have supported me in everything – and I mean, everything. From every single idea I have come up with, no matter how big or small, they have helped me get from idea to execution (though many did not make it past idea phase). They never made me feel as though there were gender roles or different expectations of me as the female in our household. More so, they have encouraged me to do my own thing, run my own race and I truly believe it is their unconditional support and encouragement that has given me the confidence to always go after what I want and believe in.

We have always been close and never really fought, and when Mom was diagnosed with Alzheimer's, our bond definitely strengthened. We came together and became each other's confidants and sounding boards. We immediately understood the importance of being one team. When something is happening to only you and your family, it is essential to be a united front. We were faced with unimaginable challenges, which understandably could have torn us apart. Of course, in some cases, we didn't agree: we had our moments but they never lasted long. We implemented ways to cope and ensure that we never let anything fester or escalate between us.

In the early days, when Greg's eldest Aaron was a baby, we would meet once a week before work for breakfast. It was a time for us to come together and be siblings but also to talk about anything that was happening at home. Mom's Alzheimer's took over our lives and many of the times we would have spent as a family were now about Mom and Alzheimer's, so it was important that we had this time, once a week, together.

I openly say that I hit the jackpot when it comes to brothers. I am immensely proud of them, mostly for how they show up every single day for their wives and children, and for Dad and me. They both possess a calmness that I truly admire and I often wonder how they can control themselves in the ways they do. I know it is something they inherited from Mom. Greg makes life look like a breeze, as if he is sailing through. Nothing is ever too much for him and even when he has a million things going on and three active children to schlep, he always has time and patience for everyone. Ricky has a tenacity that has driven him to achieve so much in his personal and professional life and he constantly shows up for his family and everyone around him. If you could sum up my brothers in a word, it would be *mensch* – the Yiddish word which means a person with integrity, morality, dignity, someone to admire and emulate, someone of noble character.

* * *

My parents were always 100 per cent devoted to my brothers and me. There isn't a thing they wouldn't have done, or didn't do, for us. Throughout our lives, I witnessed the sacrifices they made for us, doing so without any hesitation.

My parents had an established life in South Africa, including Dad's successful dental practice. But they decided to make the move to Australia because of uncertainty surrounding South Africa's future. They wanted to keep our family together and believed that, by coming to Australia, they would have the best chance of doing so. My brothers and I were young at the time – Greg was sixteen, I was thirteen and Ricky nine – so while it was sad for us to leave our old friends and uproot our lives, we quickly slotted into our new school in Sydney. We made new friends, became reacquainted with some old ones whose families also emigrated to Sydney, and joined sporting teams. Other than the challenge of being in a new country, life for us was pretty easy. But for my parents, it wasn't so simple. They had to start over, with Dad building a new dental practice and both of them making new friends and connections. Kids are so much more resilient in such situations: we can adapt and get on with things much more easily. Dad in particular struggled with all of the changes, but he kept in mind the reason for being there, for why we'd left South Africa.

The sacrifices they made exemplified my parents. How much Mom and Dad lived for their family was on display when Greg had his first child only a few months before Mom was diagnosed. The night Lee went into labour, we all rushed over to the hospital – not just Mom, Dad, Ricky and me, but Lee's family too, all of us so excited. I don't know if Greg and Lee really wanted everyone to be there, but there was no getting rid of us. We would have gone into the birthing suite and watch it all happen if we'd been allowed to. Aaron, my first nephew, and my parents' first grandchild, was born on 3 February 2011, bringing an abundance of joy and love into our lives.

While Mom's diagnosis in June that year brought the darkest times, it was also the happiest of times with a newborn, a heart-wrenching clash of circumstances. Mom was wonderful with kids due to her kind and caring nature, but she couldn't be left alone with the baby because she was already beginning to slip into the depths of dementia. It broke Dad's heart. He'd dreamed of the day they would have grandchildren, and the diagnosis was a huge blow to that dream. Initially, while I don't believe Dad was in denial about Mom's ability, he so badly wanted her to be able to look after her grandchild that he made himself believe she was capable. Sadly, however, she wasn't. It sounds crazy, an adult needing to be supervised by another adult, but that was the stark reality. No-one wanted to deny Mom the opportunity to spend time with Aaron and then later her other grandchildren, so there always had to be someone with her when she was with a baby. It was such a hard thing to accept, when all she'd wanted was to spend her days cooking for and schlepping around with her grandchildren, playing with them, building beautiful relationships.

All of the grandchildren are a blessing to us. After Aaron came Greg and Lee's second child, Dov. I remember how, on Mom's fifty-fifth birthday, Dad threw a party for Mom at home, and she was holding baby Dov and showing him off to all her friends, so very proud. We always knew Mom would make the best *bobba*. It was a role she was born for. But by the time she had two grandchildren, it was bittersweet to witness her with them. On the one hand, she was so gentle and babies naturally gravitated towards her and she would often have a big smile on her face when she was around them. But on the other hand, she couldn't enjoy her grandchildren independently. Greg and Lee would make a huge effort to ensure Mom had quality time with the boys, regardless of her capabilities. She would sit on the floor and play with them, making baby sounds, and sometimes it almost felt as though she could relate more to them than us. By the time Greg and Lee's third child, Jakey, was born, Mom had moved into her first care home. Most weekends, as I described in an earlier chapter, Greg would bring the three boys to the home to see Mom, and the time they spent there together became the foundation of their relationships.

Children have an amazing ability to make you forget about anything that may be worrying you, because of their innocence, sense of play and naivety about the world. This is why it's so uplifting to watch children interact with the elderly. Young kids are also non-judgemental, so despite Mom's Alzheimer's, Greg and Lee's kids treated her as they would anyone else. When she started losing her speech and her ability to walk, it could be tough visiting Mom, but the kids made the visits easier. When they came along, there was always physical and emotional interaction, which lent the occasion more meaning and substance. We'd often catch Mom staring at the kids with a subtle smile and a general ease about her. We also ensured that it was a fun and light experience for the children, while encouraging them to develop an understanding of, and appreciation for, those who are not well. Today, you can see the compassion that these boys have for others. Spending their formative years exposed to someone with Alzheimer's has matured them far beyond their years.

A few years after Jakey was born, Ricky and Lauren gave birth to their first child, Ali, the extended family's first baby girl. By this stage, Mom was in what would be her final home.

Every new member of the family gave Mom another reason to keep going, and the bond between Ali and her 'Buboo' was something special. Ali would climb up onto

Mom's bed or into her wheelchair and simply sit with her, sharing her crackers. It was an innocent, heartwarming time they shared together.

A person with Alzheimer's regresses and becomes more and more childlike, so sometimes we'd watch Mom and the kids interact as if they were on the same level. The kids' playfulness was matched by Mom, as though she could relate more to the kids than us. Some of my favourite memories are of the kids all rallying around Mom, engaging with her, and vice versa.

The grandchildren couldn't have come into this world at a more purposeful time. They have given Dad so much to live for as he continues to heal. He has taken on the role of both Grandpa and Bobba, picking them up from school some days, going to watch them play sport most weekends, having them over for dinner, and generally spending a lot of time with them; he would see them every day if it were possible. He always has bagels and treats for them after school – for someone who has always taken enormous pride in the cleanliness of his car, he seems amazingly tolerant of the mess they make inside it. He builds things with them out of Lego, and in summer he swims or constructs sandcastles with them at the beach. We always joke that he is a kid at heart, that maybe he missed out on some of his own childhood, so now he is making up for it. On a Friday night when we are at his home for Shabbat dinner, we often find ourselves looking around and asking, 'Where's Dad?' He is always off playing with the kids in the toy room.

In Jewish culture, there's a belief that when one person leaves the world, another enters, and that the departing person's *neshama* is passed to the newly arrived person. It's why we name a newborn after a relative who has recently passed. The incredible thing was that a month or so after Mom passed away, Ricky and his wife fell pregnant with their second child. When they told us, I knew that Mom's *neshama* was being passed on in our family. I'm not typically a spiritual person, but in difficult times, anywhere you find a sense of meaning to embrace is a gift.

When their daughter was born on 21 August 2020, Ricky and Lauren wanted to name her after Mom. They didn't want to use the exact same name, though, and decided on Isla Noa. In making their choice, they spoke with several rabbis and heard a story with a focus on two specific names, Noa and Tirtzah. Mom's Hebrew name was Tirtzah. In this story from the Torah, two sisters – Tirtzah (Mom) and Noa (Isla) – petitioned Moses to amend a law to allow property to pass to daughters and the case was brought to the Hashem and the rules were changed. The connection between the two daughters and them being mavericks was a beautiful and meaningful connection from Mom to Isla.

The Long Goodbye

The day that Isla was named in synagogue was also by coincidence the same day that we came out of our year of mourning. On that day, we had a service to mark the end of the official mourning period for Mom, which was followed in the same service by the official naming of Isla Noa. The connection between Mom and Isla was sealed, and the *neshama* tradition was continued through them.

Chapter 15

CHAI
(Life)

I can't recall exactly when I started writing about all of this. What I do remember is simply having an urge to put pen to paper; it was something I felt compelled to do. And as the words started to flow, I realised that something profound was happening. The more I wrote, the more I felt a sense of release. As I told a story, described an experience, I was able to let go of it. Writing became the only therapy I needed.

The idea of seeing a therapist never gelled with me. I do believe in them, and there were certainly times as a family when it was crucial that we sought outside help to navigate these uncharted waters, but personally, sitting down with someone to talk about what was going on had no significant impact on me.

There was a time shortly after Mom was diagnosed that I did go to see a therapist, not because I felt that I needed to, but because everyone was suggesting it and I wanted to get them off my back. When I walked into the psychologist's office, the sheer sight of it was actually more depressing than my reasons for being there. I am sure not all psychologists' offices are like that one, but it was desperately bleak. It was as if, because those who went there were depressed, the environment should reflect that. Anyway, I sat on an old couch in this poorly lit room and told the therapist exactly what she wanted to hear. After the session, there was a mutual understanding that I was not going to return. I left feeling underwhelmed by the experience. Perhaps we were not a good match, or therapy just wasn't what I was seeking at the time.

The thing is, after the Alzheimer's diagnosis, the disease had become a part of my everyday life, something I lived and breathed through Mom. I felt as though I was talking about it all the time. And if I didn't bring it up, someone else would. In the early days, my brothers and I would meet once a week before work for breakfast, to check in with one another and talk through any issues we were having. We'd also meet with Dad over dinner so we could nip any issues he'd noticed in the bud. All we did was talk about it. Eventually, not talking about it was like taking a break, grabbing a few moments to escape reality, to feel like things were normal again, even if they weren't. In addition, having already accepted the fact of Mom's Alzheimer's, I felt that nothing anyone could say to me would change the situation.

The upshot was that I didn't need answers or strategies for myself, especially not with writing as my therapy. Which is what led to another big realisation: the more I wrote, the clearer it became that my story was so much bigger than me. I knew I had to share my personal experience in the hope that it would help guide and give a sense of comfort to those who found themselves in a similar situation.

The writing process started a few years before Mom passed away. After the funeral, I took a break from it. The service and the week that followed had such a profound impact on me, and I truly found peace with my first-hand experience of death and Shiva. A few months then passed when I didn't always feel like writing, but more and more there were these times when I wanted to recall the memories, the hardships, the lessons, the challenges. I was still doing it for me, but it was as much for everyone out there who was going through the same thing or who might go through it in the future. Every time I sat down to write, I came back to the idea that it might help someone else.

* * *

After the seven days of Shiva comes Shloshim, thirty days of mourning where you go back to work but, as with Shiva, refrain from any celebrations – listening to music, watching TV and so on – and say the Kaddish twice a day. Admittedly, I did not completely observe Shloshim. A friend's wedding took place a few weeks after Mom had passed, and while I wanted to show respect for Mom, I also wanted to help my friends celebrate a very important milestone: I felt I could experience sadness and joy simultaneously. But I also understood that the loss of a loved one is a catastrophic event, and how you cannot return to normal life without processing it. The Jewish mourning period gives you the opportunity to do this. In fact, when Shloshim has been completed, there is the option of continuing to mourn for a full year.

About a month after the funeral – the final goodbye to Mom's physical presence – things generally went back to normal, or the 'new normal' as I began referring to it. While I had an overwhelming sense of comfort and support in the days and weeks after Mom's death, inevitably people had to go back to their daily lives.

They say that, when it comes to grieving the loss of a loved one, there is no clear timeline. I believe you never fully recover; rather, you learn to adapt and live with the loss. In my case, I learned to physically live without my mother, knowing that no-one in this world could replace her. I also learned that no-one can really understand exactly how you feel when something like this happens. No two experiences are the same, so no-one can ever truly walk in your shoes, nor you in theirs. All you can do is respect everyone else around you for their life experiences, and never compare them with yours. You can learn to appreciate what you have, and never forget what you have lost.

I have noticed that when different milestones come around – the anniversary of Mom's passing, or Mother's Day – I receive what can feel like pity from others, even if that's not their intention. But I don't need Mother's Day to remind me of how much Mom means to me or how much I miss her. No special day is going to make that love or hurt any stronger or weaker. It can be nice to know that people are thinking of you, sending messages, telling you that you're in their thoughts, that your loss has not gone unnoticed. And some people might need that. But I'd rather not be treated differently because I have lost a loved one, especially not out of some guilt a person has that they haven't suffered like I have. Mom always deserved to be celebrated, and she always will be. So if you're lucky enough to still have your mother here, celebrate her, shower her with love and gifts. I can handle it, I promise you. I get joy out of my friends and family members celebrating Mother's Day, because I know if my mom was here, I would be doing the exact same thing.

The Long Goodbye

The strange thing about losing someone is how it hits you at random times. On a day-to-day basis, you carry on with your life. What other choice do you have? But then, without warning, triggered by something or by nothing, you feel an overwhelming sense of sadness. It's a feeling that comes from losing someone for no good reason, a person you loved deeply, the kind of person the world needs more of.

At other times, seemingly out of nowhere, it is possible to experience a profound joy. An encounter I had in 2022 exemplified this for me. When Mom was still being cared for by Dad at home, Sheli would take her to volunteer at Our Big Kitchen (OBK) in Bondi, a community-run kitchen that makes and delivers meals for those who are less fortunate. Every Thursday, OBK had a *challah* bake, and while the dough was rising, the women would sing and dance to Israeli music. Mom loved being there; she was in her element, able to express herself without judgement. The people at OBK loved her presence, likely because Mom brought such a positive energy. The staff never made Mom feel 'less than' or incapable, but instead they engaged with her, catered to her needs, and embraced her.

In 2022, I attended OBK for a *challah* bake, and I mentioned Mom's name to the woman who was running it. Her eyes lit up like I have never seen eyes light up before. At that moment, I knew the impact Mom had made at

OBK, and that her time there had been something very special. The woman told me she was so grateful for how Mom and Sheli spent every Thursday volunteering their time to help others, and how much everyone there loved and adored Mom.

It was Mom's caring and compassionate nature that drew in Dad and made him fall in love with her from day one. She lived a life of service, whether she was serving her family, her community, her friends or anyone else in need. What a remarkable way to live. They say *tzedakah* starts at home, and there is no truer saying. Mom instilled the meaning of *tzedakah* in my brothers and me, and I only hope that I am half the woman Mom was in serving others.

* * *

The first real milestone that hit home was Mother's Day, 2020. When Mom had been in the nursing home, we'd go there on Mother's Day to celebrate with her, but this was the first year without her presence. Before Mom passed away, I'd often thought about what that day would be like. I had friends who'd lost parents, and I knew how hard those days could be for them: the in-your-face reminder of what they had lost. The idea of celebrating someone who is no longer with you may seem strange, but I think those days are an opportunity to remember and be grateful for the time you had.

That first Mother's Day without Mom, my brothers, Dad and I drove to the cemetery. What a strange thing that is: visiting someone's grave. I'd been to that cemetery many times in my life, mostly for the funerals of people who had died in old age, but sadly also for services for friends who had tragically lost their lives at a young age, and younger family members who had been ill. However, I'd never gone back to the cemetery to visit them. Yet here I was with my family, standing around the place where Mom was buried. In the Jewish religion, the coffin is buried at the funeral but the gravestone is not erected straightaway. This happens a year after the service. As Mother's Day is in May and Mom's funeral was held the previous October, we had not put up the gravestone yet, so the burial site was just covered with grass.

It was peaceful standing there, knowing that Mom was at rest, that she wasn't suffering anymore, and neither were we. It was another moment of acceptance. We all talked about Mom, our memories of her, everything she was missing out on, and the loss we shared with Mom no longer in our lives.

A few months later, on 13 July, it was Mom's birthday, and we again visited the cemetery. This is now the routine: every time Mother's Day and Mom's birthday come around, we visit her at the cemetery. We haven't given up celebrating Mom. We've simply changed the location of the celebration. Maintaining these dates as significant moments in our lives, even if Mom isn't physically here anymore, is so important to all of us.

Before we knew it, it was time to decide which gravestone we wanted for Mom: what kind of marble, what colour, what shape. The choice was an important one, as this would be the monument we would be visiting for the rest of our lives. We went back and forth on what stone it should be, eventually deciding on something elegant and uncomplicated – we still wanted the best for her. The next time we visited the cemetery was for the Hakamat HaMatzevah (unveiling of the monument). In Jewish culture it is a religious obligation to place a marker at the grave of a loved one with family and close friends joining you – although not nearly as many as at the funeral. A rabbi conducts the ceremony and it feels like an extension of the funeral. The unveiling of Mom's gravestone happened on a chilly Sunday morning and it was another experience where I got to feel a sense of comfort, sharing the moment with two of my closest friends, those who had known Mom the longest.

When Alzheimer's took over Mom's life, she could no longer directly share in our celebrations. She couldn't come to dinner with us adults on our birthdays or be at the kids' birthday parties, nor travel with us; not only did she miss out, we did too. But it was always important to us that she was included in some way, and it still is. For one thing, it reminds the kids of how proud Bobba would be of them for their achievements. We often tell the children that if Bobba was here, she would be at every single soccer match, the same way she was at every one of our sporting games when we were kids, and even as adults. She was everyone's biggest supporter, and just because she isn't here now, we don't stop reminding everyone of the role she played, and the significance she held, in all our lives.

* * *

There have been many times when I have thought, *If only Mom was here.* I'm still quick to remind people what Mom would have thought about all sorts of things if she were here now. Her opinion still very much matters, and it's important for me and my family to remind ourselves that what we do still reflects on her. Not that Mom was one to make anyone feel bad about anything, but she had high standards and values, and I believe it's important we maintain them in the way she would have expected us to. Mom didn't get mad about many things, but if Dad was out of line, for instance, she would be the first to pull him up – if not with words, then with a stern look. We were always very aware when we'd done something she didn't agree with.

I feel the loss of Mom strongly every time we go on a family holiday or there is a wider family celebration, particularly involving Dad's side of the family. Before we emigrated to Australia from South Africa, we travelled to Perth to visit my uncle and cousins. I was nine years old, and it was the first time I remember our two families coming together. Every trip since then has been memorable; we always have a blast. I often recall the bond between Mom and her sisters-in-law – the three of them really had the best of times. But while Dad and his brothers make a great effort to see one another, and they are definitely among my favourite occasions, there is still a hole there, and we all feel it. I look over at my aunts and it saddens me that Mom is not there with them. She is the missing piece, and there is no replacing her.

We still count ourselves lucky to have incredible reasons to come together as a family. One was in November 2022, when my grandparents had their seventieth wedding anniversary, and Dad, my brothers and I travelled to Perth to celebrate it. A few months later we all returned to Perth for my cousin's bat mitzvah (marking a girl's twelfth birthday). I remember sitting in the function room, listening to my cousin giving a speech, and looking around the room at so many familiar faces. Every occasion like this, no matter where we are, includes some recognition of Mom in a speech. She is always a part of everything we do.

As I sit here writing this, we are planning a trip to Perth for my *oupa*'s 100th birthday. One hundred years old! It's an incredible milestone. But then, my *oupa* is a phenomenal man. Most days he swim laps in a pool, and his mind is so sharp; other than losing his hearing, he is in impressive shape for someone of that age. With a grandparent reaching a century of life, I can't help but think about the fact that Mom passed away so young. My *oupa* has lived almost forty years longer than Mom, and he has nine grandchildren and sixteen great grandchildren.

The loss hits me the hardest on Jewish holidays, which I find really difficult to celebrate without Mom. My memories of these holidays are strongly centred around family, which is the reason why I always loved this part of the year. When I was growing up, Mom owned these times. She would be busy in the kitchen for weeks in advance, preparing all the traditional food, which generated such a strong feeling of Yiddishkeit. Even after I moved out of home, I'd always return to my parents' home for these occasions. Nowadays, however, Mom's loss feels so strong that everything is different, and I can't quite enjoy the holidays as much as I used to. When someone passes away, you don't always realise straightaway all the small things that have been stolen from you.

As I reflect on the past few years since Mom's funeral, I am proud of how my family continues to keep Mom's memory alive. How Dad continues to talk about Mom and their life together with so much love and respect. It's important that we continue to acknowledge Mom in everything we do. While life moves forward without Mom physically, she is always with us spiritually. How my brothers constantly talk about Bobba to their kids, making sure she remains a constant in their lives, and teaching them as much about her as possible. How she will always hold a special place in our family despite her physical absence.

Chapter 16

ED'S STORY

I have taken great comfort in connecting with other people who have experienced the strain of caring for someone with Alzheimer's first-hand. It's not that people in general can't provide understanding and support, but Mom's Alzheimer's was unlike anything else I had ever before experienced, and I did not expect friends and extended family members to fully comprehend what was going on – the same goes for any significant upheaval that someone else has been through but I haven't. So when a few years into working with CHeBA, I got an email from Heidi Douglass asking if she could introduce me and my brothers to a man whose mother had developed Alzheimer's and didn't know anyone else going through the same thing, we said yes without hesitation.

In the first instance, Greg met with Ed for a coffee in Sydney's CBD, and then Ed and I spoke on the phone and texted for a while before meeting up in person one day down by the beach. My family had already navigated a lot of stages of the disease, which meant I could empathise with what Ed was handling for the first time. Our experiences were not identical, because no two situations are the same. While essentially anyone who has Alzheimer's will lose their memory, the timeframe, pathway and behavioural effects are different for each person: some people become withdrawn, some are aggressive, while others become forgetful but do not change in character. Regardless, we had a lot of common ground to share and much to talk about, especially in the initial period after Mary's diagnosis.

Those first few years are some of the hardest to deal with because it's when you're first confronted by significant changes in the dementia-affected person, including their inability to do things for themselves. And as the carer of that person, your life changes significantly too. Ed was working in Sydney when his Melbourne-based mother, Mary, was diagnosed, and he started spending more time in Melbourne to be with her. In an ideal world, we would just stop our lives and look after our loved ones full-time when they fall seriously ill, but the reality is that this often isn't possible – we still need to go to work, earn a living and continue building our lives.

And sometimes it may not be what's desired. That's a horrible situation to grapple with, knowing you want to be with your loved one and care for them, but also realising that you might not want to become a full-time carer because it's too much for you to handle. I had that thought initially and felt very guilty about it, but I came to learn that there is no shame in not wanting to care for your parents full-time and instead opt to spend quality time with them. I would've done anything for Mom or Dad, so I certainly didn't want to wash my hands of any responsibility; rather, I was being realistic and honest about what I could handle as an individual.

Mary was formally diagnosed in 2016, but Ed can track the first signs of her illness back five years before that. He was already living in Sydney then and his mum would always call on his birthday. But this year, for the first time, she forgot. He called her the following day and set up the conversation by saying, 'Aren't you forgetting something?' She didn't know what he was referring to. When he said it had been his birthday the day before, she said she'd known that and had simply been waiting for him to call her. Mary's response seemed intended to cover up her forgetfulness, showing how resourceful someone can be in that situation. There were conversational issues, too. Ed and Mary would talk about golf and she would say she couldn't remember where her golf clubs were – Mary hadn't actually played golf, or even owned a set of clubs, in forty years.

At the time, Ed did think incidents like these were weird, but because they occurred only periodically, he never thought they meant anything. If anything, his reaction would be more annoyance than concern – something he now feels bad about, knowing his mother had actually been experiencing the early stages of dementia.

Ed also struggles to comprehend why his mother developed Alzheimer's in the first place. He recalls that his mother was always very active, both physically and mentally. She would walk everywhere, and she continually worked as a bookkeeper. She also did a number of courses over the years and generally kept herself stimulated through a variety of hobbies and pastimes. Furthermore, his mum wasn't a drinker, she stuck to a pretty healthy diet, and to the best of Ed's knowledge there was no history of dementia in his family. The only known risk factor that stands out is that Mary was once a smoker; it was a different time back then and smoking was a very accepted part of our mothers' generation.

In the wake of the diagnosis, while Mary was still living at home, Ed had organised for up to five carers to come at different times every day to help look after her. However, it got to the point where she needed someone to be there around the clock; she simply couldn't be left alone. An example of the problems that arose was Mary's decision to start smoking again, even though she hadn't done so for many years. Ed tried to stop her, even lying to her when he visited and she tried to light up: 'You've just had one,' he'd say to her. At the same time, Ed felt like he was denying Mary one of her civil liberties by not letting her smoke, which left him conflicted. Perhaps fortunately, Mary soon just forgot about it and never again tried to smoke. Incidents like these prompted Ed to make the difficult decision to move back to Melbourne to care for Mary in her own home.

Ed held off putting his mother in a home for as long as he possibly could. It was absolutely the last decision he ever wanted to make. But he hit rock bottom, reaching the point where he was physically unable to look after her anymore on his own. Looking back now, Ed doesn't believe his mother would still be alive if she hadn't gone into a home.

Mary now lives in a home in Melbourne. The carers there have told Ed how people in the home who never or rarely receive family visits seem to decline much more quickly. So when Ed is in Melbourne, even if he's flat out with work, he takes his laptop to the home in the middle of the day and sits there doing his work while keeping his mother company. It was during the COVID-19 pandemic, however, that Ed demonstrated his understanding of the importance of human connection to people with Alzheimer's – something Professor Henry Brodaty had also emphasised to him. At the height of the terrible lockdowns in Victoria, he fought hard to be able to keep visiting Mary, unable to bear the thought of not seeing his mum. When this appeared to be in jeopardy, he decided to pull Mary out of care and move back to Melbourne to look after her full-time. Ed knew there was a certain risk of him giving his mum COVID, but he also knew there was a 100 per cent chance of her declining during this time if she was left entirely alone.

The first stint was seven weeks straight, after which Ed returned his mum to care. But that was only the first of numerous lockdowns, and each time, Ed would again discharge his mum from aged care and look after her himself. For most of 2020 and 2021, Ed ended up personally taking on his mum's care, for varying periods, within a few weeks of her being re-admitted to the home. He admits that he suffers post-traumatic stress disorder as a result of that time, when he stretched himself to the end of his emotional tether. He knew that emotionally and physically he just couldn't keep doing it, but he felt selfish for even thinking that. For those two years, Ed had absolutely no emotional relief: he alternated between being the good son who was under immense stress trying to look after his mum, and the bad son who kept sending her back to aged care.

It was horrific, and having had this first-hand experience of being a primary carer, Ed says he wouldn't recommend that a family member takes on this kind of responsibility.

* * *

After Ed and I had connected, we stayed in touch. Ed soon became involved with CHeBA too, and with his strong corporate network he remains a huge asset to the organisation. He demonstrates a passion and desire to make a difference that I can completely relate to. When you realise the prevalence of Alzheimer's, your only hope is that a cure will one day be developed, so that no-one else will ever have to go through it.

Over the years, Ed has run the Sydney Marathon to raise money for CHeBA, successfully leveraging his corporate connections to do so. He has also supported WipeOut Dementia at Bondi Beach and the annual CHeBA lunch on World Alzheimer's Day in September. I look forward to those events so I can meet up in person with Ed and also PJ Lane. Our individual passion for CHeBA and what it strives to do was what bound us together initially, but there is so much more to our relationships now. It extends beyond CHeBA and research into healthy brain ageing and is a lifelong commitment to advocating for the rights of all people with dementia.

This is why being selected alongside Ed and PJ as CHeBA Change Maker Ambassadors in 2022 was one of the greatest honours of my life. It was at the World Alzheimer's Day lunch, when I was sitting at a table with my brothers and various other fundraisers, that the announcement was made, and I immediately felt this great pride flow through me. The Change Maker Ambassador role is one I have taken very seriously since that day.

* * *

In the past dozen or so years, the number of people I have met around my age who have parents with Alzheimer's is frightening. How is it that so many of our parents have developed this disease, often at such a relatively young age? As I now know all too well, the notion that Alzheimer's only occurs in old people is about as far from reality as it gets. I am constantly hearing about adults in their fifties and sixties being diagnosed with the disease. In some cases it's hereditary; in other cases the exact cause remains unknown. And more and more people appear to be getting diagnosed due to concussions and other kinds of repeat trauma to the head. Whatever the reason, it's a devastating diagnosis to receive. In Australia today, 244 people are being diagnosed with dementia each day. When it comes to early-onset dementia, 28,000 people are currently affected, and this is expected to rise to over 40,000 people within the next quarter-century – and this can include people in their thirties and forties.

When you live and breathe the impacts of this illness, you start seeing things from a very different perspective. When it strikes someone you love, your exposure is heightened greatly, and so is your awareness of what's at stake. You realise that without properly funded research, the future looks pretty bleak. That's why the inroads being made by organisations like CHeBA are so important.

So is the adoption of brain-healthy habits. This can't be delayed, because you don't know what your brain will be like in the decades to come. You need to embrace a healthy lifestyle right now, ranging from physical fitness to keeping your brain active. Living a healthy life should be the status quo – rather than an aspiration, it should be normalised. It involves simple things such as not smoking, not drinking too much alcohol, eating healthy food, exercising regularly, socialising frequently, and keeping your brain stimulated. If people who work long hours, or are largely inactive or have a bad diet start to do something about these lifestyle factors, it will be a game-changer for them and society in general.

* * *

A common theme among those who need to place a family member in a home is the challenge of navigating the aged-care system and accessing the necessary care options for people with dementia. Ed has experienced it, PJ has experienced it, and I have experienced it. You can't even say that the system has been broken because the truth is that it has never worked. It is a bleak, arduous and unforgiving process where, in the depths of great physical, mental and emotional stress, you need to make significant decisions about someone's life and complete mountains of paperwork. And the reality is that the only people who have actual experience in the sector are financial advisers, because the decision-making mostly comes down to what you can afford and/or what government support you can get. It's a labyrinth of asset management, legalities and waiting lists, none of which serves the person with dementia or their family – it only weighs them down with even more stress.

Everyone I've spoken to who has gone through this process has had an awful experience. As a primary caregiver or immediate family member, you are at your emotional wits' end, yet you still have to deal with the complexities around getting your loved one into care. The system is definitely not designed to cater effectively to anyone who suffers from dementia.

Carers can also encounter difficulties in dealing with the diagnosing and treating doctors, be they GPs or geriatricians. You would think that, on the whole, they would be able to help you with the next steps, but that is not always the case. Both Ed and I have encountered medical professionals who have no information about assisted care or specialist living facilities, or who struggle to admit that your options largely come down to what you can afford. There is often a terrifying gap between someone being diagnosed and them receiving appropriate dementia-specific care.

Dementia needs to be treated more seriously and comprehensively by both medical professionals and the aged-care industry. The needs of a dementia patient are vastly different to those of an elderly person who requires assisted living. It's rare to find carers who are specifically trained in dealing with dementia, and even in a dementia-specific facility, the care provided is often not specialised enough. That's why people like my father and Ed have had to employ extra resources, at their own expense, to give their loved ones the daily care they need, over and above daily necessities such as bathing, eating and sleeping.

* * *

Today, Mary is still capable of some enjoyment of her life, and Ed remains a devoted visitor, although Mary does tend to spend most of her time in her room. Ed feels like, on balance, they are in a good place. Seven years on from the official diagnosis, he is still able to have a conversation with his mother. But will the required level of care be there when her condition worsens? There are already signs that Mary's health is deteriorating. She used to ask when she could leave the home and he would have to talk her out of it. Now, she doesn't ask anymore, which is sad as it represents a decline.

Ed tries not to get too caught up in this sadness or in anticipation of potential negative scenarios the future may bring. Instead, he tries to enjoy the situation for what it is. But it is hard for him, having given up the responsibility of primary care for Mary. It would be easy to get angry at the world for what has happened to Mary but Ed prefers to focus on how we can create a brighter future for dementia sufferers through research and advocacy for healthy brain ageing.

Chapter 17

OTHER STORIES

Mom's story didn't have a happy ending. We weren't able to 'save' her. But we were able to give her the very best care, and to make her life as comfortable as possible, given the circumstances. And I still have hope for the future, for people who will sadly develop dementia. I have faith that with education and awareness, we will all take our own health more seriously. I don't mean that we should live our lives wrapped in cotton wool, but rather own our choices and make healthier ones. Every day we are faced with decisions: whether to move our body, to eat healthy food, to be social, to contribute to society. One thing I have personally vowed is that I will do everything in my power to avoid becoming a burden on society. Whatever I can control of my own health, I will. I have witnessed what happens to someone with Alzheimer's, and to put it bluntly, there is nothing humane about it. This is no way for anyone to live. So if I can avoid it, I'm going to.

I also hope that, through continuing research into brain ageing, we can unlock ways of being far healthier and living longer. If we all continue to support this research, one day there could be a clinical trial that will reverse the effects of brain ageing. We must keep hope that there can be more medical breakthroughs.

Along with improving health outcomes, I hope that we change the stigma around Alzheimer's, and improve how we care for and treat people who have this illness. I was simultaneously fortunate to come across the kindest and most caring people while Mom battled Alzheimer's, and unfortunate to be confronted by people who lacked knowledge and compassion. As a society, we have so much to learn about Alzheimer's and its growing prevalence, and so much work to do.

I have connected with many people over the years who have been affected by different forms of dementia, people who I may not have otherwise met if it weren't for my own experiences. I see this as the silver lining to what I've been through. I wish none of us had to go through what we did, but every single one of these people is striving to make a difference for those with dementia, and that has made a truly awful situation meaningful.

* * *

I met Reidy in 2019 while I was working on an event called Red Bull Defiance at Mission Beach in Far North Queensland. He was one of the competitors. We got to talking about dementia and discovered that both of our mothers suffered from it. Little did I know that only six weeks later, Mom would pass away, bringing her battle with Alzheimer's to an end. Reidy and I still cross paths through work and down at the beach, and I know he is very supportive of dementia research and the cause in general. I continue to find it comforting to talk to Reidy about his mother, who is still alive, and feel that we're on exactly the same wavelength.

Reidy's mother, Trish, was born in 1947, one of four kids. She met Reidy's dad almost fifty years ago, married him and started a family in the eastern suburbs of Sydney. Reidy has two sisters, and all three were active kids. It was around six years ago that Reidy started to notice little changes in Trish, such as that she would forget things, but he didn't think much of it at the time. Then, one day, she got really sick and became delirious, which is when she was diagnosed with dementia.

Trish is now in a late stage of dementia and lives in a nursing home. When she was first diagnosed, she moved to Lake Macquarie to live closer to Reidy's sisters, who became her primary carers – particularly the eldest, Kirsty. Trish's husband would help too, but there wasn't much he could do as he himself was quite elderly. When he passed away at the start of 2023, Trish declined even further. Her family had always sworn they'd never put Trish into a home, but with the grandkids struggling to understand what was going on with Trish, and her behaviour more affected by her illness, they had to. It was the best thing for everyone.

When we were chatting one day, Reidy mentioned how Steve Jobs, in a Stanford University commencement speech, talked about looking back into your past and connecting the dots. Looking back at his mum's life, Reidy reckons she always knew she was going to get dementia, which is why she did so many things to try to fight it off. She had nursed her own grandmother through the disease and would always talk about how horrible it was. She never wanted to give up smoking, though, which Reidy thinks is because she figured she'd rather die from smoking than from dementia.

Reidy brought up another idea that I have thought about many times. When you have first-hand experience of a family member with dementia, you develop strong feelings about it. Inevitably, you wonder about whether it could happen to you, and what you would do if faced with that. Knowing what I know, I would want to be put into a home so my family didn't have to look after me, and I would strongly consider voluntary assisted dying. I know that's very confronting for some people to hear, but if you'd also cared for someone you loved who had Alzheimer's, you'd understand. Reidy feels the same way that I do. He's already had conversations with his wife about not wanting to end up where his mum is now.

Reidy is also quite open about how tough a time he's had with his mother. Part of him wants her around as long as possible, but it's hard because it's like the real her is already gone.

There have been many times when he's visited his mother and gotten nothing out of it, and he feels so guilty about this. Visits where his mother has been unable to communicate have been especially hard. Hearing Reidy express the feeling that sometimes you don't want to visit someone who can't give you anything back, which I felt on occasion with Mom, gave me some comfort. He knows that when Trish is gone, he will wish she wasn't, but it doesn't make those visits any easier.

One time, Reidy took his mum out on a cruise on Lake Macquarie. It was a gift from his wife, who thought it would be a nice thing for mother and son to do together.

But spending hours with someone who can't converse with you, or who gives you the same response no matter what you say, is very difficult and can just leave you feeling lonely – which is what happened to Reidy. He ended up feeling even sadder and was left wondering what good came out of such efforts.

You learn to pick your battles with Alzheimer's. Initially with Mom, we fought for her to still do certain things, but after a while, we realised there was no point and it only made things harder for us. Reidy experienced this too. Some behaviours caused by dementia, especially in relation to personal care and hygiene, can be very hard to accept, especially as they are so out of character for the sufferer. This can be really distressing and difficult to witness and deal with.

Reidy is worried about what the future might bring, especially as he has three young kids. Ultimately, we both hope a cure for dementia will one day be found, and that is why research is the most important thing we can invest in. The money raised for such research is vital, and we need to keep working away at this. Reidy and I also agree that much more education is needed about dementia, about what it is and how it might be prevented or slowed.

Once, when Reidy was telling me about the tremendous toll grief took on him, he quoted Queen Elizabeth II: 'Grief is the price we pay for love.' No words have ever been truer. When caring for someone with dementia, you are faced with so many emotions you are not prepared for. Some of them can shock you. Because of the cruelty of life with Alzheimer's, at times Reidy and I both wondered if our mothers might have been better off at peace.

* * *

I was introduced to Anthony Scotts by Heidi from CHeBA. Anthony, a commercial furniture manufacturer in Sydney, is one of the team captains for WipeOut Dementia and has raised a significant amount of money for research. What struck me the most from our meeting was Anthony's passion for looking after his family. Knowing how difficult the role of a carer is, it is inspiring to hear about Anthony's dedication to his loved ones. But what also resonated with me was Anthony's conviction that, with an Alzheimer's diagnosis, there is no hope, only time. Those caring for someone with Alzheimer's don't have the luxury of hope, because as yet there is no cure, nor a promise of one. That means the time remaining for our loved ones becomes the priority.

Anthony lost his dad to Alzheimer's after a twenty-year battle and is now looking after his sister, who is ten years into her Alzheimer's journey. Going through it once is bad enough – I cannot fathom going through it twice. Anthony comes from a big, loud and loving family – he grew up with seven siblings. He remembers how, when he was only a few years out of school, things changed for his dad after the collapse of his business. Anthony describes his dad's business loss as a massive upheaval for him, and wonders if the stress of it was a catalyst for, or at least a contributing factor in, what followed.

It was when Anthony's father was attempting to fulfil a lifelong dream of travelling around Australia that his wife began noticing a decline. At around 3 p.m., a witching hour would start, with Anthony's dad getting tired and grumpy. Then he started getting clumsy in the kitchen and leaving the gas cooker on, and then his memory began to fade: he'd try to remember names and couldn't get them out. It was a very slow, drawn-out deterioration that eventually led to Anthony's father being moved into a home, with his wife visiting for three to four hours every day to help with cooking and anything else that needed to be done.

Primary carers typically take on the role of advocate for those they care for, making sure they're being looked after properly in a facility. That means being aware of when the person is being washed, and fed, and given medication, and engaged in activities. Staff in nursing homes, who have a thankless task, can struggle with these aspects of care. Anthony would sometimes make a surprise visit to his father's nursing home and find him still in bed in the late morning, rather than showered or bathed and up and about.

Anthony was the last person in his family to see his father alive. His dad was covered in bed sores and clearly at the end of his road – there was nothing more anyone could do. Anthony tells me, 'One thing with health: if there's hope, go all the way, but if there is no hope ...' He remembers the smorgasbord of pills his father would have to take, the tiredness that would weigh down his father every afternoon. Before it came to that, Anthony explained that his father would implore him, 'Son, don't ever put me in a home.' Anthony had to live with the guilt and sadness of going against what he knew were his father's wishes, but which could just not be accommodated.

The gravity of this is unfathomable to most. And when it happens a second time, it seems almost unbearable. Anthony's sister Gillian, the eldest of his siblings, is sixty-nine years old, developed Alzheimer's around ten years ago, and now resides in a home in Mosman. Her Alzheimer's began showing itself through memory loss. While her husband was at work, she would just walk the streets, visiting the same coffee shop and repeating the same activities. She didn't understand what money was for. She burnt herself in the kitchen. There came a time when she couldn't be left alone at home, and Anthony and his brother-in-law had to make the call to try and get her into a home. It wasn't easy. Gillian's husband had to fight to get her on the National Disability Insurance Scheme (NDIS), which took two years to deal with her case. He described the process as 'disgusting'. Gillian ended up sitting in a room with contractors who would ask her, 'Have you got Alzheimer's?' To pose that question to someone who is four years into the illness shows a deep disconnect between the reality of dementia and those who carers are supposed to trust. Anyone who knows anything about the disease would never ask a sufferer a question like that. How could someone so far into the disease respond to that?

When Anthony told me that, I reflected on how lucky my family was to be able to afford to put Mom into the homes we did. I don't take that for granted at all. I know the financial strain it put on Dad, and I'll be eternally grateful to him for the personal sacrifices he made to enable it. But I often think about what we'd have done if we hadn't been able to put Mom into a home. Where would she have gone? How would we have been able to take care of her? Hearing about Anthony's encounter with the NDIS made me extremely angry at the system, especially at how people with no real experience of an illness are making decisions that affect people's health and livelihoods.

Eventually, Anthony and his family did find a home for Gillian, which they are very happy with. But it is still hard. Within two weeks of being moved into the home, Gillian escaped. She is a very elegant lady and when she walked out of the home, no-one took any notice. She ended up walking to Collaroy, fourteen kilometres away. One of Anthony's other sisters eventually found her at three o'clock in the morning, in the area where she had grown up. Anthony thinks that maybe she was trying to get back to what she knew, to what was familiar to her.

Anthony shared a photo with me of two of his sisters who care for Gillian a few times a week, sitting with her outside on a bench. He said, 'It hits me for six. They are just sitting there, but it's so special.' As he showed me the photo, I had flashbacks of similar moments with Mom: images of her and Dad sitting together, of Dad holding onto her. Then Anthony revealed that Gillian had since slipped into what was close to a vegetative state, and she was confined to a wheelchair when not in bed. She had been having fits and needed to be medicated, and now she mostly just slept, her personality and quality of life completely diminished.

Anthony is well aware that there is a distinct thread of Alzheimer's in his family – it has affected not just his sister and his father, but his father's mother as well. But like me, he has made the decision not to be genetically tested, explaining that life would never be the same if he knew. Anthony is, however, well versed in what he needs to do to have the best chance of avoiding Alzheimer's. Enough sleep, good fitness and healthy eating are key, plus not spending your days worrying about everything. 'Dwelling gets you nowhere,' he tells me. 'Live for today and look forward to tomorrow. That is the most important thing to come out of this … Live life to the max.'

Anthony tries to do as much as he can. He has done the gruelling Bondi2Berry bike ride a couple of times, raising a huge amount of money in the process. One of the wonderful things about events like this is how people come together for such a worthy cause, many of them having had their lives touched by Alzheimer's. Individual stories and experiences differ but often there's a sense of hopelessness. But it is this feeling that inspired us to want to do something about it. We are all championing awareness and raising money for research, because that is the only way we can make a difference. 'We all know there is no cure,' says Anthony. 'But so much of it is about the carer at the end of the day. There isn't much we can do about the patient – make sure they are happy, in a stable environment. But it's the family around them that needs the help and support.'

Anthony and I reflected on how young Mom was when she was diagnosed, and the fact that Gillian wasn't that much older. People are increasingly being diagnosed with dementia in their forties and fifties. The healthcare system has a lot of work to do to get up to speed with this ever-worsening situation. In the meantime, says Anthony, he will never give up raising money and awareness wherever and whenever he can.

* * *

When I sat down with Nick Noonan and heard the story of his dad's struggle with Alzheimer's, it drove home how, with dementia, your mourning period begins when your loved one's personality or behaviour starts to change – they forget a name, they find it hard to walk or speak or recognise you – and then never stops. When Nick spoke about his father, and tears started to roll down his face, I needed to keep it together, but I could feel my heart breaking all over again. It was a stark reminder of how cruel this disease is, and what it takes from a person and those who care about them. Simultaneously, however, there was joy in hearing about the kind of person Nick's dad was, and how much love and joy he brought to the people around him.

When Nick's father started exhibiting signs of dementia and was subsequently diagnosed with the disease, Nick withdrew inside himself. He didn't speak to many people about what was going on, not even other family members. He describes it as a kind of paralysis. Nick's dad had been so vibrant, the leader of the family, and when he could no longer play that role, it made things really difficult. Nick suddenly found himself having to take on new responsibilities all while grieving the changes taking place. He told me: 'When you think about the role that a person plays in the family, someone who is such a big personality, well known, well liked, full of life, all those things, then it's like you're mourning someone that is still alive.'

When I ask people when they first started noticing signs of dementia in their loved ones, I almost always get the same response: many years before the diagnosis. This realisation only comes with reflection, with looking back and joining the dots – at the time of these incidents, it's rare that anyone understands what's happening. For Nick, whose family grew up and mostly lived in Cronulla, it was when his father became forgetful in the business he ran, which eventually led to him making some irresponsible decisions that were very out of character for him. When these uncharacteristic behaviours escalated, Nick's mother took her husband to see a doctor and have some tests done, leading to an initial diagnosis.

For a while, the diagnosis was trivialised with off-hand comments like, 'Ah, that's the old dementia again.' But everything changed when Nick went to the geriatrician with his father in 2013 and witnessed the basic testing his father did. He recalls the geriatrician asking his dad, 'How did you get here today?', 'What day is it today?', 'What suburb are we in?', 'Can you count down from 100 by threes?' and 'Who is the prime minister?'. Nick's father couldn't answer any of these questions. It was at that moment, while sitting there stunned, that Nick realised the extent of what was happening to his dad.

The damage being done by Alzheimer's was hard for other people to grasp, too. Nick describes his dad as having a vibrant personality and being well known in the local community. He had this manner about him that was very likeable and showed his integrity. And he also had the ability to disguise what was going on. When he was walking around the neighbourhood or at the beach, people would often say hi to him and, being charismatic, he would greet everyone. The frustrating thing for Nick was that, during these fleeting interactions, people would think that his dad was doing fine. They would often approach Nick and say they had seen his dad and he was really well. It got to the point that Nick even started second-guessing himself and the diagnosis: was it actually that bad?

It's no wonder Nick had a hard time grappling with this new reality. He was the one having those more intimate interactions with his dad at home, when it was evident that he was not OK, when it was a struggle to look after him. Other people were not exposed to what Nick saw day in, day out.

Nick's father remained at home for about five years post-diagnosis before the idea of being cared for in a home was seriously discussed. He was still good for the most part, especially physically. He'd always been a fitness freak, always tackling new types of training and drills, and he carried this through into his later years. He was still running, playing golf, heading down to the beach in the morning. But he was also getting on trains and then forgetting where he was going, and there was growing concern about his ability to drive. Nick remembers how his father loved the surf so much, and one time Nick and his dad were getting ready to go out among the waves and his dad forgot what to do with his leg rope. It was such a small thing, but he was so confused that Nick couldn't let him paddle out.

Nick recalls the experience of putting his dad into a facility as a very difficult one. They found an aged-care home near to where they lived, opposite the beach, and on the day of the move, Nick had to trick his father by dropping him off there and telling him it was temporary while his wife was away. 'Driving him up there was awful,' says Nick. 'I said he was staying for the weekend – it was all set up ... as a short-term stay, [but] with a long-term view.' Nick continues: 'He lasted one day. He didn't want to be there. It was hard ... such a build-up to making that decision and emotionally preparing ourselves.'

When you have gone through the emotional roller-coaster of preparing to send a loved one into care and it doesn't work, what do you do next? You have to deal with what many people in this situation have described to me as an absurd aged-care system. Making it even more difficult was the fact that Nick was largely solely responsible for arranging his father's care, and had to try to navigate this complex system by himself: figuring out the costs, where to go, what resources were available. Needless to say, there were a few false starts. Nick recalls going to see one place that seemed to fit the bill and then discovering it had a really long waiting list. What was he supposed to do while waiting for a bed to become available?

Nick finally got his dad into a care home with a dementia ward, which he said was confronting. The ward housed people with varying degrees of dementia and a myriad of other conditions. His dad was a very gentle man, so being in a home with other people who were aggressive as a result of dementia was hard. He couldn't really interact with anyone else, and again he lasted a single day. Nick received a phone call informing him that his dad had escaped. The home simply told him, 'We can't find your dad. On looking at the security camera, it looks like he followed the cleaners out and left the premises.' This resulted in a fifteen-hour search that was covered by various news channels, and which was a traumatic time for Nick and his family, who feared the worst.

Nick's father was found late that evening. He had managed to travel thirty kilometres from the nursing home before spotting a car that resembled one he'd owned a decade earlier. He must have thought it was his car and, as the car was open, he proceeded to get in and put it into gear. The car rolled down a hill and stopped in a gutter. Someone heard the commotion and came out to find Nick's dad in a state of utter confusion; he contacted the family by dialling the number on his ID bracelet. When Nick was finally reunited with his father, he found him sitting having a cup of tea, unaware of what had just transpired. This incident prompted the nursing home to upgrade its security system, but it should never have gotten to that stage.

Nick was able to transfer his dad to a home closer to where the family lived, but because the COVID pandemic had begun by then, there were various restrictions on visiting residents. Those last few years were awful for Nick. Someone who has dementia needs to see their family, to interact with other people, in order to have some quality of life. Denying access to them only increases the heartbreak for all involved, robbing people of time with someone they love – time they will never get back.

One way in which Nick brought some light into all this darkness was to expose his father to as much music as possible. Nick's dad may not have been able to talk by then, but when Nick played music, his father would sing along, even if he couldn't exactly recall the words. Nick also took him to music-filled movies such as *Rocketman* and *Bohemian Rhapsody*, and those were fond times.

Throughout it all, Nick just kept going. 'You have a choice to fall apart but you can't,' he says. 'I had a young family and had started a business, compartmentalising my life ... I was in robot mode.' Nick says this meant he didn't really discuss the situation with anyone, but at the same time he struggled with the lack of support for him as a carer, resenting other people for not reaching out and seeing how he was doing. He says, 'You are keeping everything together and you think, *When is it my turn to have a breakdown?*'

Nick was riddled with guilt. He envisioned people judging him for putting his dad in care. The guilt extended to his mother. She was still so young, and Nick didn't want all that sadness to dictate the rest of her life. He wished he could devote more time to her, but he simply couldn't be there all the time. There was anger there, too. He said people always asked about his dad, but what about his mum? She was suffering as well. He felt like saying to them, 'You have her number. Call her and take her out. Ask her how she's doing.'

Once Nick's dad was finally in stable care, he went downhill quickly, soon becoming immobile and non-verbal.

Nick refers to dementia as a death sentence and he is spot-on, because there is no hope of recovery. So when his dad passed away, it was bittersweet. It was Christmas Day 2021, and Nick had taken his dad out of the home to be with his family for the morning. Nick remembers him looking so small and vulnerable, sitting there in his wheelchair, a stark contrast to the man he'd always been. He got to spend that morning with all his kids and grandkids, but the next day he slipped into a coma-like state. Nick stayed by his side up until he passed on 30 December.

No-one likes to talk about death, but what you realise when you are faced with it is that our society needs to normalise the idea of death from a young age. It is unavoidable: when you are born, there is only one certainty in life, and that is that you will eventually die. Most of us who have witnessed a loved one go through the agony of dementia have talked about death extensively and subsequently end up thinking about how we want our own lives to end. We have had very real conversations, and we've had to become comfortable with some uncomfortable ideas. Many of us never want to be put into a home, or have our life prolonged if we don't have any quality of life or dignity, because that is not the kind of existence we want for ourselves.

Nick and I talked deeply and openly about our feelings on this issue. It is typical for someone who has, or has had, a family member with dementia to continually contemplate their own future. It always weighs on you, the knowledge that this might be something that happens to you.

Nick's dad was a professional sportsperson who experienced two decades of high-impact rugby league, when the game was at its most brutal and concussions weren't yet considered overly dangerous. But there is now a new narrative around concussions in sport and brain-related diseases, and Nick's family donated his dad's brain to further the research into this area. For Nick, the idea that his father's Alzheimer's was fuelled by repeated head injuries, while not something to feel good about, gives him some belief that he can avoid a similar diagnosis, as he doesn't play rugby himself. He may eventually discover he has been unlucky in the genetic lottery, but for now, he just concentrates on remaining active and healthy, on being social, on having an enriching and fulfilling life.

* * *

It was important to me that I not only share my story in this book but also some of the stories of others, as each one is unique and important to know. While we were all dealing with dementia in some form, our experiences are different and each one of us endured varying struggles across the many challenging situations we were faced with.

Despite the differences, there were so many commonalities and things that understandably no-one who has not been affected firsthand would understand, and personally I found comfort in knowing I wasn't alone. Through these stories that I have been able to share, I hope other people can find comfort and resonance for their own experiences.

Chapter 18

PREVENTION

There is no cure for dementia, not yet. There are some drugs that show promise in slowing down the deterioration, but they come with side effects and are costly. What we do know with certainty is that prevention is our greatest form of defence against this disease. As I have said many times throughout this book, healthy brain ageing is something we should all be personally striving for.

Elderly Australians are the fastest-growing segment of the population, which is why CHeBA has undertaken the Sydney Centenarian Study. This project explores the genetic and environmental determinants of extreme longevity. The study examines the cognition, health, care needs, brain structure and genetics of Australians aged ninety-five years and older. It's an interesting notion that someone can live healthily until they are 100 years old, yet a much younger person's life can be cut short so dramatically.

In my family, as I mentioned in Chapter 15, we have our very own living centenarian: my *oupa*, Dad's dad. So we find ourselves contemplating the differences between his long, healthy life, and that of Mom's. My *oupa*'s father passed away in his early fifties, so it seems unlikely that my *oupa* inherited his longevity. Genetics may have played a part, but more compelling reasons for his life span are the decades of physical exercise (he still swims and lifts weights); of maintaining a sharp mind, constantly learning and educating himself; and of social connection and the general desire to always stay busy, stimulated and explorative. His health and longevity are a reflection of the lifestyle choices he made throughout his life, which we have come to learn are fundamental to preventing diseases such as dementia.

Dementia affects over 50 million people worldwide, a number that is predicted to increase to 150 million people by 2050. Every three seconds, someone in the world develops dementia, and research tells us that two out of three people globally believe there is little to no real understanding of dementia in their countries. The stats are frightening, but so significant that we cannot shy away from them. In addition to the human impact, the cost of dementia is huge.

The estimated worldwide cost of dementia in 2015 was US$818 billion. It is now estimated at US$1.3 trillion, and is expected to rise to US$2.8 trillion by 2030.

You simply can't ignore the impact of dementia in Australia. It is the second leading cause of death of all Australians, and provisional data is showing that it will likely be the leading cause of death within the next decade. It is already the leading cause of death for women and is the single greatest cause of disability in older Australians (those aged sixty-five years or older). It is also the third leading cause of disability burden in this country.

Professor Henry Brodaty told me about a first-ever national study that was launched by CHeBA in September 2023 to investigate whether we have experienced a generational change in brain health and risk factors for dementia in Australia over the past twenty years. It is important to know this especially as there are now more people aged sixty-five and over than there are aged fifteen years and under. Our population is becoming older, and we can't ignore how this will impact the incidence of dementia. In 2023, it was estimated that more than 400,000 Australians were living with dementia. Without a medical breakthrough, the number of people with dementia is expected to double by 2058.

What I find even scarier is that, in 2023, it was also estimated there were more than 28,000 people living with early-onset dementia, a number that is expected to rise to more than 42,000 within thirty-five years. Further, it is estimated that more than 1.5 million people in Australia are involved in caring for someone with dementia, and two in three people with dementia are thought to be living in the community; that is, outside of a dedicated care facility.

As is hopefully clear from the story this book tells, it's not just the person with dementia who is impacted by the disease but also their family, friends and carers, the healthcare system and the wider society and economy, and this cannot go unaddressed.

* * *

Alzheimer's disease is the most common form of dementia. It is a progressive condition that advances slowly, and which is caused by the build-up of abnormal amyloid beta proteins in the brain – it is these toxic proteins that are thought to be damaging to brain cells. This damage can accumulate twenty to thirty years before clear symptoms present themselves.

Professor Brodaty explains that we have the ability to identify people who are accumulating these toxic proteins and provide drugs for them. These people may not yet have dementia but rather evidence of Alzheimer's pathology in the brain, which can be identified through specialised

PET scans. Brodaty describes it as nuclear medicine, where an injected radioactive tracer attaches to abnormal proteins which light up on the PET scan. If you have these proteins, it doesn't necessarily mean you will end up with dementia, but you will have a greater risk of developing the disease. It's likely that a third of people over sixty-five years old will light up with amyloid-PET scans with these proteins.

According to Brodaty, two new antibodies have already been approved for dementia treatment by the US Food and Drug Administration, with a third to be approved soon – and approval in Australia to hopefully follow. He explains that these drugs appear to remove the amyloid beta protein from the brain fairly well within six months, and definitively within eighteen months. The person will still decline, but more slowly than if they were not taking the medication. The long-term goal is to identify people who are developing dementia early on and give them these drugs before they start showing clinical symptoms. For this to be effective, a patient would need to get tested by having either an amyloid PET scan or a lumbar puncture to confirm that there is amyloid on the brain. However, this is not straightforward, as these procedures have known side effects. In addition, the antibodies themselves can cause micro-haemorrhages and swelling of the brain, and they're pricey. Brodaty suggests that, as with many other diseases, treating dementia will probably involve a multi-drug approach, as is the case with illnesses like leukaemia and tuberculosis.

CHeBA has spearheaded research that spans the whole spectrum of dementia diagnosis and treatment, from understanding the molecules that go awry in the brain through to improving diagnoses by GPs and the care offered in nursing homes. Another aspect of this research is epigenetics, where changes in the functioning of our genes is investigated, specifically those prompted by changes in the environment. Genes can actually be switched on or off in ways that are very unhelpful for us, which is why epigenetics has become a strong focus of research. Dr Karen Mather, Senior Researcher at CHeBA, clarified to me that 'genetics' refers to the study of genes and DNA and how it varies from individual to individual, and heredity, while 'epigenetics' refers to mechanisms that work independently of the DNA sequence and affect the degree to which a gene is turned on or off.

As we age, we naturally accumulate damage to our DNA. Dr Mather explained that our DNA is continuously harmed by exposure to environmental factors, like ultraviolet radiation, X-rays and industrial chemicals, as well as chemicals and toxins generated by the body. Much of this damage can be corrected, however. Dr Mather stresses that a healthy lifestyle is the best way to promote healthy brain ageing, reinforcing what Professor Brodaty advises.

Eating well, being physically active, learning new things throughout life, being socially connected and having a purpose are all hugely important. Dr Mather also reiterates the importance of not smoking and minimising alcohol consumption.

CHeBA is leading the way in dementia research, and collaborating with groups all around the world. Currently, CHeBA is working with four other countries to develop a post-diagnostic care package to help dementia sufferers take control of their lives, to empower them and their families and carers. The ideas behind Forward With Dementia are to help people with dementia and carers understand how they can live positively with dementia, to educate medical professionals about identifying and managing dementia, and to educate the public about what someone can do if they get that diagnosis.

Researchers are also looking at heritability to assess the relative importance of genetic versus environmental factors for different dementias and brain shrinkage. According to Professor Brodaty, our brains start shrinking after the peak age of twenty (on average), with the rate of shrinkage increasing significantly post-sixty. This highlights the urgency of a good education early on in life. Researchers believe that different areas of the brain are subject to different levels of heritability, meaning that the relative contributions of genetics and the environment may differ across brain regions.

This leads us to the question: what is it in our environment that we can control? While we can't reverse a decline in cognitive ageing in relation to dementia, we can slow down the rate of decline, and maybe even delay its onset. Professor Brodaty believes that if we attend to the primary risk factors – not using your brain enough, physical inactivity, midlife obesity, midlife high blood pressure, type 2 diabetes, head injury and hearing loss – then perhaps we can postpone an onset of cognitive decline. Avoiding these risk factors allows us to build up a buffer against any pathology that threatens to develop in the brain.

I asked Professor Brodaty what we should all be doing to reduce the likelihood of developing dementia. The list below applies even if the dementia has a genetic basis – as Brodaty explains, we can't change our genes, but we can influence how they work.

1   Keep physically, mentally and socially active.
2   Exercise for at least half an hour a day for at least five days a week (although an hour would be even better), mixing aerobic and strength training, and incorporating balance training.
3   Get a good education, especially early in your life.
4   Exercise your brain. This means going beyond stretching your brain by doing the likes of crosswords or Sudoku puzzles. It means learning

a new language, learning to play a musical instrument, and generally doing things that are challenging rather than repetitive.

5　Be socially active. There is evidence that people who are more socially connected have less risk of developing dementia.

6　Get your blood pressure checked regularly, and have it treated if it is high.

7　Maintain good nutrition. The evidence points to the effectiveness of the Mediterranean diet, but other healthy diets can work well too. The main thing is to incorporate lots of vegetables, legumes, grains, almonds, walnuts, extra virgin olive oil, moderate amounts of fish and dairy, and only small amounts of sugar and red meat.

8　Protect your head from physical injury.

9　Address hearing loss, such as by wearing hearing aids. There is evidence that hearing loss overtaxes the brain and in time weakens memory.

10　Avoid obesity. It is important to watch your weight, particularly in midlife (it doesn't seem to be a risk factor after the age of seventy-five).

11　Diabetes is associated with obesity and it is an independent risk factor for dementia.

12　Avoid air pollution and high levels of carbon monoxide.

The World Health Organization has released its own guidelines on *Risk reduction of cognitive decline and dementia*, which can be distilled into a dozen recommendations that echo Professor Brodaty's list:

1 Be physically active.

2 Stop smoking.

3 Eat a balanced diet, like the Mediterranean diet.

4 Drink alcohol in moderation.

5 Do cognitive training.

6 Be socially active.

7 Look after your weight.

8 Manage any hypertension.

9 Manage any diabetes.

10 Manage any cholesterol.

11 Manage depression.

12 Look after your hearing and manage hearing loss.

* * *

These are the things we can do to minimise our chances of developing dementia. But if dementia is present, what are the warning signs? What should we look for, and how do we know when these signs indicate dementia?

One warning sign is short-term memory loss. This can involve people repeating themselves, including asking the same questions over and over; not recognising familiar faces; getting lost on familiar routes; and having trouble finding the words for things – for example, someone saying 'the thing you write with' when they are referring to a pen. It is normal to forget things – we all do it from time to time. It's when it becomes progressive and other people start noticing that an assessment is needed. Another sign could be not understanding concepts that are a bit more complicated, or not being able to follow the plot of a movie. Another potential sign is when a person's personality changes and they become more irritable, or perhaps apathetic – they lose their spark, their initiative, essentially their starter motor.

I also spoke to Professor Brodaty about one of the most important things I learned through my lived experience of Alzheimer's: that just because a person has been diagnosed with dementia, it doesn't mean they're no longer able to enjoy spending time with loved ones or doing things they love. Brodaty confirms this, people can live positively with dementia. Using examples such as playing tennis or the piano, or going for a walk along a beach, he says that, while the person with dementia may not do these things as well or as easily as they did before, they can certainly still benefit from doing them.

He also explains that dementia doesn't simply wipe out the entire functionality of the brain, and that it's important to build on what *is* working to compensate for what *is not* working well. This became evident to me throughout Mom's journey. We learned to employ various strategies when her memory became an issue. Technology can help with this; for example, a smartphone alarm can be used to prompt someone to take their medication. Maintaining quality of life should be a principal goal.

I often wonder why there is such a stigma associated with dementia, and I mentioned to Brodaty that I believe this is largely due to a lack of education. But he suggests there is a double stigma: 'Anything to do with ageism, which is quite prevalent, has a stigma, not just in general society but amongst doctors themselves and other health workers. And secondly, mental health has a stigma.' He suggests that dementia, being an ageing problem affecting the brain, frightens people for these reasons.

Professor Brodaty's hopes in relation to dementia rest on three things:

1   There are things we can all do now to delay the potential onset of dementia, as described in detail above, and we should all be doing them.
2   Better diagnostic tools are beginning to emerge, including blood tests for Alzheimer's disease, although these are not yet used in clinical practice.
3   Ideally, medication that is specific to all forms of dementia, especially Alzheimer's, is key.

* * *

Mom's Alzheimer's came as a complete shock to my dad, my brothers and me. As far as we are all aware, there's no history of Alzheimer's in our family. Mom's dad did die in his fifties from a rare form of cancer, but that may or may not be a factor. I often wonder if it was down to bad luck, bad genes, lifestyle, environment, or a combination of these. We may never know the truth. What we do know is that possibly less than 1 per cent of Alzheimer's cases are caused by a single genetic mutation that is transmitted through families, and where symptoms usually present in a person's forties and fifties. This is early-onset familial Alzheimer's disease (EOFAD). Three genes have been associated with EOFAD, and if a parent has a mutation in any of these genes, any child of theirs has a 50 per cent chance of inheriting the same mutation.

Other genetic variants can increase or decrease a person's susceptibility to Alzheimer's, but they do not cause the disease. One example is the apolipoprotein (APOE) gene. The presence of the APOE 4 gene variant is associated with an approximately three-fold increase in the risk of Alzheimer's disease; having two copies of this gene variant is associated with an eight to twelve-fold increased risk.

The presence of the aforementioned genes can be revealed through specific tests. Some people decide to undergo these tests. My personal choice is to not get tested – in this, I am unequivocal. I do live with the fear that I will develop dementia. Whenever I forget something, or have a period of brain fog, which I know is normal, I can't help but stress about it, overthink it and analyse it, and wonder if it's happening to me. But still, I do not want to know if I am a carrier of one of those genes. I also do not know what consequences a result would have on any application for life or health insurance. Instead, for the past decade I have focused on making healthier choices. I have seen someone's life taken from them. I have seen what it looks like for someone to live with this disease. So living a healthy, active lifestyle is really my only choice.

Beyond this, regarding a disease that currently presents little to no hope, I now look to the future with a renewed determination. I want my voice and my story to offer guidance to those who will sadly be affected by dementia. I want to be a friend in what can be a lonely and difficult time, a source of comfort and empathy when the world feels really small and you feel helpless. My ultimate hope is that no person ever feels alone when navigating the world of dementia; that no-one with dementia is ever treated differently or as 'less than' someone who does not have the illness; and that we as a community, as a nation, stand up for each other in the face of the adversity that this disease inflicts. We can't stop dementia entirely, but there are things we can control: we can ensure that every patient receives quality treatment, that there are adequate care options available, and that no family has to suffer when trying to care for a loved one.

My deepest hope is that we find a cure or, better still, a way of preventing dementia. I dream of this. Death is one thing we cannot deny will happen to all of us, but so is life. So while we are on this earth, let us all strive for good health and happiness.

Chapter 19

MOM'S DIARY

Mom started seeing a psychologist in August of 2011, soon after she was diagnosed. During the sessions, which would take place at home so she remained comfortable, Mom would often write down in a diary what she had done on a particular day, to remind herself of these things and also provide an opportunity for her and the psychologist to discuss them. Soon, she was also describing how she was feeling and writing about events more broadly. By the middle of September, however, Mom had stopped writing in the diary herself and the psychologist had taken over maintaining it – Mom could no longer write and needed someone else to do it for her.

These diary entries provide important insights into how

Mom was dealing with dementia. So many things were changing, every day, and Mom was simply trying to make sense of it all. These entries also revealed to us, her family, what we were doing right and what we could improve.

I think Mom's insights are relatable and deserve to be shared widely. They offer small lessons about the mind of someone dealing with Alzheimer's, and how a family might navigate this together.

17 August 2011

Home this morning – cleaned out cupboards for Keri, did some shopping, got caught in rain.

Dad came home. Brad and Michael came over with Chana. Had a great time.

18 August 2011

Went to Double Bay to deposit.

Bought some fruit and veggies.

Popped into Grandpa Moses to collect what I needed.

Met Cheryl at Espresso. Had a good chat with Cheryl.

Came home at lunchtime. Decided to make soup. Got all the ingredients and cooked for tonight as we have Yahrzeit tonight. Ray and Cheryl are coming to spend time together. Unfortunately Harold does not join us. Went for a walk – did it slowly due to stitches. All organised for tonight. Must light the candle.

20 August 2011

Had a lie-in this morning – freezing weather.

Did some chores at home.

Walked down to the shops. Bumped into Brenda and Daniel.

Got lunch for Dad – chicken salad. Waiting for Dad to come home.

Dad and I went for a walk to the Police Station. Came home, had lunch and relaxed. Out with Jacobsons to a Thai place in Rose Bay.

22 August 2011

Had my stitches out. Sandy came through to the east to spend the day with me.

Evelyn arrives from Perth. So excited to see her.

23 August 2011

Amanda and Marcelle came through to the east.

Evelyn and I caught the bus to the Junction. Met up with Shilana at the Junction.

Walked with Lynn and Ev to Double Bay. Had coffee and then walked back home.

25 August 2011

Thursday, went to play with Aaron – lots of fun. Lee cooked and I looked after Aaron.

26 August 2011

Spent the morning with Ev. She left – took a cab to the airport. Had a great time with her. Went to Ray and Che for Shabbas.

30 August 2011

Meeting Bev at Espresso for coffee.

Did my walk with Lynn to Double Bay.

Had a good walk. Home now. Ricky at home too.

4 September 2011

Out with Lynn and Stan for dinner to a fish place.

Went on our boat to the fish market. Had lunch on the boat.

Had a good time.

Father's Day.

At this point, Mom stopped writing entries and her psychologist took over. This meant the entries started taking a different form. The diary became more of a resource for Mom to express her feelings and work through them with the psychologist. It was also there for us to read and get an understanding of what was going on with Mom. She was OK with us reading it – I think it made her feel empowered to talk about her feelings, which were often confusing to her. It helped her make sense of things in the early days, when it would have all been so confronting. I can only imagine how scary it was for her to not feel fully in control of herself.

In the diary, the psychologist talked through any issues Mom was having and broke them down for her. For instance, there was one comment about Mom looking after her grandchild when Lee went back to work. She expressed to the psychologist that she didn't feel she could do it alone but would need someone there with her. She was very intuitive. She knew her boundaries, and as much as she would have loved to do it by herself, it simply wasn't something she could handle alone.

Reading through the notes, you can see that Mom did keep things to herself. She never truly expressed to us everything she was feeling – she wasn't able to organise her thoughts to articulate them all, but neither was she one to complain or burden us. For these reasons, I am grateful she had the psychologist to confide in.

19 September 2011

Shared baby news.

Terry shared her anxiety about a visit to St Vincent's this afternoon. As the day has progressed and the arrangements are clear and supportive, Terry felt better.

Man who has a private taxi will fetch Terry at 4.30 p.m. He will take her to St Vincent's and up to Drs rooms and stay with her while she meets Martin [my dad].

The Long Goodbye

'I couldn't go on my own, too overpowering. I can go and ask to find my way, but I am anxious. I'm worried I would have to call a cab, get there myself.'

'I used to be positive and I am trying to get that back. I need a definite sure arrangement.'

'In my anxiety, I panicked, had a little cry. I composed myself. Sat down, relaxed, played on the computer. I left it, then felt better. I also went for a short walk. I don't mind that I don't know him, as long as he fetches me, takes me to the doctor's room and stays with me until Martin comes to meet up with me.'

'Crying is not always bad, I learned that. It is like I am asleep and tears come out and I feel better after.'

'Greg and Ricky can calm me.'

'My daughter Keri is staying here. She runs early at the crack of dawn and I only see her a few minutes here or there. We are managing perfectly with everyone in the house.'

'The doctor's appointment is a check-up. I've been getting on with life, so nothing to ask and nothing to tell him.'

'Dinner tonight: nephew Neil is here for two days for a conference. He is also staying here. The house is full. He is from my side of the family. He has 3 kids.'

Re: Lee-Anne, Greg and baby Aaron. 'I love being with them but do not want to be left alone to babysit. We had a lovely day. We go most nights at 5 p.m. to bathe him.'

'If I was not with Greg, Aaron and Lee-Anne when Martin is not with me, who would I have to be with? I could walk baby Aaron up and down the street but taking the pram is a problem for me. I feel I want to be cautious.'

'My kids read what we discuss and I feel they know what is going on.'

7 November 2011

1   *Wedding*

Where there was set seating and someone wanted to change seats. Martin (who was protecting Terry) suggested that they keep the seats as they were explaining 'Terry has Alzheimer's'.

Terry was upset as she felt she was at a wedding to enjoy herself and there was no need to discuss the diagnosis.

Terry sees that Martin was being protective but feels the explanation was not necessary.

2   *Saturday night dinner with friends*

In the intimacy of friendships, Terry felt very comfortable to share with her friend that she has Alzheimer's and to discuss it with her.

'I am very happy to be open but in the right place and I need to feel comfortable. It bothered me because it was at the wrong place. I said I would be open but sometimes it just doesn't feel right.'

'I appreciate they were trying to help me – but they didn't help.'

'I am now reacting more strongly than I did in the past. Before, I wouldn't open my mouth and talk – now I say what I think. When I was told about the Alzheimer's, I didn't accept it, now I do.'

'I have been shy and reserved. I used to sit back. Now I say what I feel and think. I am better than I was.'

My family and I often speak about how Mom used to be so reserved and never really expressed an opinion. Ironically, before Alzheimer's stole her ability to communicate, it seemed to give her a voice we never knew existed. She said to the psychologist that when she first received the diagnosis, she didn't accept it, but a few months later she did. She had always been innately shy and reserved and would often sit back, but then she began expressing what she felt and thought. In some ways her Alzheimer's empowered her to assert herself more often. It certainly wasn't in her nature, but perhaps it was an aspect of her personality that was always there, just suppressed.

23 January 2012

Recap holidays.

Driving – rationally, everything is accessible and on the doorstep, but emotionally, while Terry says she has no choice and will accept that she cannot drive, it is hard to realise that she can no longer drive and how this will impact her independence. Her feelings are facts.

'It's hard going as there are lots of things I cannot do and I don't want to have to depend on others – I want to be normal and myself.'

'At breakfast, Ricky suggested that I do volunteer work. Everyone makes suggestions and means well but I cannot do new things, or be in a strange situation. I just don't know – it feels overwhelming. I don't feel like I haven't got enough to do. I have my house to get organised and I walk. I feel everyone else feels that I need to be doing more. I cannot start new things and I also wouldn't know where to start.'

'My eating has changed. I eat less – I was always fussy. I enjoy eating at home and I don't like mounds of food.'

30 January 2012

Terry wants and needs honest explanations and discussions, as they are less hurtful or worrying than when she sees something and doesn't know why.

Terry feels that sometimes everyone is not sure what she can do or where the gaps are – but she wants to be included in the discussion.

'I don't want to be the one sitting on the couch and not in with them. It feels easier if they talk to me.'

The psychologist explained that we were all learning in this situation and we needed to keep sharing what we felt. She expressed that Mom was a wise and caring person who saw everyone in her life differently but sensitively. Mom tried to understand their point of view and she was generous in her acceptance of their position.

6 February 2012

1   Terry told me about Aaron's afternoon tea that she enjoyed.

2   Playing tennis – great suggestion.

3   Meeting with the Dementia Specialist – Terry was concerned she didn't recall everything and we discussed that in future at such meetings, someone should write points so we can revisit the discussion.

4   Talked about the suggestion that Terry do volunteer work. This feels too much for Terry to do at this stage.

   a   To go with a strange person

   b   To a new place

   c   And alone.

5   We discussed 'long days alone'.

Things to do:

Outside home

• Walk alone

- Walk with friends
- Go to Coles
- Walk to water
- Get a Freezochino
- Lunch with friends

Inside

- Cook
- Read
- Washing / ironing
- Computer

13 February 2012

Terry started knitting and it was easy and just came to her.

Talked about ID disc on her watch, just with her name on it and a phone number, obtainable from Alzheimer's Australia or a jeweller.

Chatted about 'the help' and the Kindle.

5 March 2012

Discussed the week.

Talked about knitting.

Terry is enjoying knitting, though casting on and off is not automatic. If Terry gets stuck, let someone correct it but NOT teach her. Knitting is to do at home to enjoy and pass the time.

The Long Goodbye

2 April 2012

Good chat, all seems on track.

Spoke about:

- Selwyn's visit
- New walking routine
- Tennis
- Greg and Lee sold their apartment
- Gorgeous Aaron being sick and his milestones
- Terry is enjoying knitting

Note: to leave knitting for me to fix if Terry needs help. She will call me if she wants me to come past and help her.

23 April 2012

Friday night was relaxed. Aaron was up.

Terry told me about the trip to Hawaii. Lots of photos.

30 April 2012

Discussed weekly routine. Terry likes arrangements and 'time out' so she can do things she wants to do.

Discussed:

- Pilates class and the challenge of following instructions
- Breakfast with the family
- Trip
- Knitting

14 May 2012

1   Terry shared Mother's Day. We talked about her muffins.

2   Seeing the professor today. Terry discussed her worry not knowing how she was getting there.
Suggestion: night before write out the plan for the day – the appointment and how Terry will be getting there to meet Martin.

3   Back to knitting.

4   Talked about a common connection and she recalled her father and brothers – but couldn't find the connection.
Terry, Raymond, Harold Jankelowitz
Father: Phil Jankelowitz
Some connection but she is not sure
Dianne married Colin – her mother was a Jankelowitz – all related
Big family – 9 children, twins passed away
Terry was a flower girl at Diane and Colin's wedding
Small world – Terry made the connection

24 June 2012

Terry and I discussed the ID bracelet. Terry has the bracelet on and it will just be there as security.

Note:

Terry mentioned the discussion – an idea put forward about having a driver to take her places. Terry does not feel this is something she needs or wants. She feels independent to walk to Rose Bay or wherever she needs to go – and if she has to go to a specific place (such as the doctor), she is happy to have someone take her.

Terry felt one day last week, one of the days was long and she was bored – but this doesn't happen often.

Terry is comfortable with the way things are (weekends are a bit busy) and likes it when people visit her and they go out.

6 August 2012

Discussed appointment with the professor.

Suggested:

- Weight-bearing exercises
- Zoloft

Discussed Caz – Terry is looking forward to meeting her on Thursday and is keen to experiment with the scrapbooking.

Socially, 'girls calling' feels a bit hectic at times, but having said that the outing with Sheli worked well.

Friday – terrible weather but Terry said she managed to do all her shopping and said it was not as bad as it looked. She was pleased she did it independently in her time.

Talked about Olympics, and Ricky and Greg training for a marathon.

20 August 2012

Shared scrapbooking session. Terry is enthusiastic about it and feels really good that Caz considers her confident doing the album.

Her routine is working and good for her.

Monday – psychologist

Tuesday – walks with Lynn

Wednesday – sees a friend

Thursday – Caz comes over for scrapbooking

Friday – chores and spends time with Sheli

Weekends are very busy!

She also had a massage which she thoroughly enjoyed and we should make this a regular thing.

At this point, Mom had been meeting with her psychologist for a year. Mom would often knit during these psychology sessions as a way to keep calm and to make them feel less clinical. She had completed knitting a blanket, which took seven months, and she and the psychologist were now thinking about the next blanket she would knit.

27 August 2012

1   Blanket complete and just needs satin border.

2   Started knitting new blanket.

3   Reviewed routine. Caz is a wonderful 'find' and her involvement doing scrapbooking is excellent.

4   Zoloft seems to be 'on track' and doing what it should.

5   Discussed weekend of Yom Tov plans.

3 September 2012

1   Blanket finished. Terry and I went to the newsagent to choose wrapping, ribbon and a card and wrapped the blanket for Aaron.
Exciting achievement and rewarding project. We have already started the next blanket.

2   Debriefed weekend. Lovely small Shabbat and Father's Day picnic in Rushcutters Bay Park.

3   Terry needs more wool, if anyone can take her; any colour will be good. Not pink!

10 September 2012

Arrived, Terry was watching Serena Williams in final so lost track of time – opened the door at 9.10 a.m. (I called Martin as no-one was answering).

Debrief week

1   Giving of blanket.

2   Scrapbooking – absolutely enthralling and exciting. Terry is looking forward to being with and learning from Caz and doing albums.

3   New blanket started.

29 October 2012

Discussed trip to Perth.

Knitting.

Chatted generally.

I will call Martin re: colour of the wool to get.

Also, if someone can access light weights for Terry.

Research is indicating light weight training is positive.

5 November 2012

- Terry and I debriefed about the week.
- Lovely news about Greg and Lee-Anne's new house. Terry explained to me exactly where it is.
- Discussed scrapbook and doing one for every child.
- Aaron's 'new tricks'.
- Perth trip.

My discussion with Martin re: end of year visitors. Very effectively communicated and all resolved.

Blanket for the new baby is progressing.

Ricky's purchased weights with Terry.

Tennis started again.

3 December 2012

Terry shows me pictures of Aaron on her iPhone.

Shared the delight and was able to accept photos to share the experience.

2 squares knitted this week and now that we know Lee-Anne and Greg have a boy we have started the 2 blue balls of wool.

Terry discussed early morning Bris on the North Shore, 5.30 a.m. wake up and preparation.

Tues afternoon hair colour and blow dry.

Terry explained to me exactly where the hairdresser is and how to get there.

Worked out from August 2011 – August 2012 = 1 year, August 2012 – December 2012 = 4 months.

I have been seeing Terry for 16 months.

Terry shared albums she has been making with Caz. They are excellent.

7 January 2013

Terry shared the news of the engagement breakfast.

Debriefed December visitors, activities and weddings.

Continued knitting – she is almost finished (I had to correct one error but essentially continued as usual).

Terry shared the pain and discomfort in her feet. She says today it has settled down.

Talked about Keri's trip.

Lee-Anne and Greg's imminent move.

Grandchildren's progress.

25 February 2013

Discussed meeting with the professor. Terry hates the quizzing and testing. She feels she is coping with Alzheimer's but hates the tests.

Terry told me about blood tests. Medication seems to be the same.

Talked about extra support and maybe filling lonely hours.

Terry has quiet times but does not want more support yet.

Talked about routine.

Started new knitting project. Terry knits very easily and proficiently.

Takes longer to open the door these days – I need to ring more incessantly. Terry doesn't always hear the ring.

8 April 2013

Wedding in December at Four Seasons.

Dress: she bought one in Double Bay. Nice dress to have. Showed me a photo of it.

Ricky and Lauren are planning the wedding, looking for a place to live. Lots to do.

Scarf almost finished.

Scrapbooks are excellent.

Talked about Bondi Pizza outing and appointment with the professor.

Terry told me her brother is coming from South Africa.

Knitting:

Terry and I have evaluated the knitting.

Initially Terry was very anxious, made errors and was worried about knitting.

Then we ensured we had two things we were working on, so if Terry made a mistake she could continue.

Now she has almost done the entire scarf.

To date Terry has completed:

- A blanket for Aaron
- A blanket for Dov
- Scarf for Keri – almost finished

We are planning the next project.

Chatted about Pilates in the evening in Rose Bay – Thursday night with Ricky, Keri and Terry.

29 April 2013

1   Discussed long walk with Lynn but wasn't sure if they walked to Vaucluse, Camp Cove or Dover Heights. She was confused.

2   Terry mentioned Perth – but wasn't sure when the trip was planned.

3   Knitting going well.

4   Friend is not coming today but Alice, another friend, is coming. She is helping today.

6 May 2013

Debrief of the week:

1   New memory album

2   Shabbat – big with family

3   Went to the St Ives Fair

4   Introduction discussion of Joyce [a carer employed to
    help Mom]. Terry will meet her with an open mind and
    see how it goes

5   Knitting this week – Terry did quite a lot independently

6   Terry said she spoke to Lynn about the last walk – too
    long, too hot and did not have water. Now walking to
    Double Bay again

7   Guessed all Greg's friends' names and needed help on
    some of the friends' partners' names

13 May 2013

Had a long chat about Joyce. We both agree Joyce is lovely
and good to have around. At this stage, Terry does not want
it to be organised or to be 'walked' but is happy for Joyce
to come, get to know her. Then take it from there, build a
relationship.

Terry told me about the wedding meeting for Ricky –
music, etc., lovely meeting and being included and
atmosphere of wedding.

Discussed Mother's Day and massage as a gift.

Talked about new neighbours, rudeness, smoking, being loud and aggressive.

Terry was unsure of the time Alice was coming and chores she needed to do and called Martin (I had to help her with the number).

Suggestion: Martin, put your number on speed dial and write it down.

1 July 2013

1   Terry told me about the fall in Perth. Also about Ev and the trip.

2   Discussed wedding and progress. Looking for a dress. Ricky busy organising shirts.

3   Lee-Anne and Greg almost ready to move.

4   Joyce was 'not what Terry enjoys'. She is an adult and does not want to be organised.

5   Knitting continues.

6   Debriefed weekly routine.

Observations:

• Weights

• Facial expressions intense

• Answers are shorter

7 July 2013

1   Terry was much happier with her appointment with the professor. She was not tested. He spoke to her

pleasantly and it was a friendlier encounter. She was sure Martin had spoken to him before, but she was pleased about it. She said maybe one change of medication, but no other major changes. She just wants to be normal and be able to make her own choices.

2   Knitting 2nd scarf, almost complete and one for each of the girls – Keri, Lee, Lauren.

3   Birthday – party and all preparations and feelings about it.

4   Weekend – house full and lovely with 'Aaron's special garden spot' – 'Grandpa where are you, we need to hurry up, lots of work to do'.

5   We have been knitting for 18 months – great achievement.

6   Ricky's birthday yesterday at Bronte – Lee and Greg didn't come to breakfast as they were having portrait photos.

7   Terry and I had a very relaxed, productive hour.

29 July 2013

1   Knitting.

2   iPad – Terry couldn't remember the password; she tried her birthday and could not type in her email address.

3   Disorientated initially.

4   Challenged with words today.

5   Looked at birthday photos.

6   Tennis.

2 September 2013

1   A bit of a challenge to get the lights on.

2   Knitting.

3   Discussion of Father's Day at Watsons Bay and friends' son's engagement party.

4   Caz and albums – Terry feels she has had enough of doing albums. Loved it initially, really likes Caz, but is bored with the activity.

5   *Boolkas* [cinnamon rolls] with Sheli and Cheryl – most enjoyable.

6   Really looking forward to day out on the North.

7   Yom Tov plans.

30 September 2013

1   Knitting.

2   Debrief of weekend – fun run to raise money for charity organised by Ricky, Keri – friends and family involved. Successful day and amazing experience.

14 October 2013

Talked about 'walk' for CHeBA.

Read article and discussed it. Really positive experience for Terry, proud of everyone.

Knitted.

21 October 2013

1   Terry showed me the magazine article about CHeBA walk. She is so animated and proud of Keri, Ricky and Greg re: the walk.

2   Talked about visit to the professor. Terry says she is a different person, and visits are no longer stressful. She said he was happy and encouraged her to keep playing tennis.

28 October 2013

Discussed going to the Rose Bay Fair on the weekend, visiting Lee at her stall.

Tennis – planned a game for this week.

Going to work with Dad and felt sick and needing to lie down.

Arrangements today with someone from the north.

Lynn is still away and Sheli is back from London.

The Long Goodbye

11 November 2013

1   Terry had a sore back and headache when I arrived.

2   Opened the buzzer for me today.

3   At about 9.40 a.m., she stopped knitting and said
      she felt her body turn to ice, she then felt warm and
      needed to sit quietly. She had a drink and sat quietly,
      periodically describing her sensations. She says it has
      happened before.

20 January 2014

Wedding and visitors debrief.

   Edge of irritability – mild.

   Terry says at times she feels like a 'little girl'. She loves
everything she does with Sheli.

It was agreed that the psychologist would come back in
February, but this is the last entry we have in the book.
It was in October 2014 that we moved Mom into a care
facility, with preparations beginning a while before that.
It was not an easy decision. In some ways it felt as though
we were giving up. I was for it – I knew that we could not
provide the care she needed anymore, and Mom would be
in better hands with experts, people who could give her
the attention and support she needed from a carer. And
Dad, my brothers and I could visit her as her family and be
truly present.

* * *

I hadn't read Mom's diary entries since before she passed –
I had actually forgotten that she had kept a diary. Only
a few months into writing this book, I was chatting to
Greg and the diary was mentioned. I was intrigued, and
so found it and began reading. Immediately, it was a stark
reminder of the first few years and how much transpired
and changed with Mom in that time. It's easy to forget the
small yet significant details of Mom's journey, the internal
battles she would have faced trying to understand and
navigate what was happening to her. I am grateful she had
an outlet, something and someone to express her feelings
to. It is a glimpse into the mind of someone going through
the early stages of Alzheimer's and, in some ways, the only
true insight we have into what Mom was going through.

The diary entries are an important part of her story,
a true and real indication of the struggles, sadness,
loneliness and frustration she experienced, but also the
moments of joy that Mom had in those early years. It gives
me hope that from this we can learn a little bit of what a
person with Alzheimer's is going through. How scary and
confusing this time would have been for Mom and how
we can support and treat people going through this. At the
time she wrote these diary entries, we were all on a journey
of discovery. Each day we were faced with behaviours

and challenges for the first time. I am hopeful that my experience paves the way for the next person to approach their own situation with more knowledge and insight into what a person with Alzheimer's is going through.

ACKNOWLEDGEMENTS

As with most things in life, I never stop to acknowledge my achievements. There has always been this urgency to move on to the next project. But today as I sit here and reflect on the past eight months, of which I devoted every spare moment to writing this book, I am going to stop and take a moment.

This book has never been about me. It may be my story, but the purpose of sharing it is so much bigger than me. I have an overwhelming sense of gratitude for being given the opportunity to share my story with the purpose of helping others and advocating for those who cannot speak for themselves.

To my immediate family – Dad, Greg and Ricky – the journey hasn't been easy. Four years on, we are still navigating the aftermath of a hurricane that could have torn us apart, and in some ways changed us forever. It is no secret that I have put my brothers on a pedestal. To me they are the greatest human beings and there is no-one else who I think of more highly. Thank you for your unwavering support and for allowing me to share our story, and for your contributions. Not only do I gloat about having the best brothers in the world, but everyone who knows you agrees with me. Dad, where do I begin? Throughout my life, you have always told everyone how proud you are of me. Everything I do is to make you and Mom proud. Regardless of how ridiculous my ideas are, you have supported me every single time. I know that you were hurt more than anyone, and you're still hurting. Your love has no bounds and your devotion to Mom is by far the greatest thing I have witnessed. I promise to carry on Mom's legacy for the rest of my life.

To Aaron, Dov, Jakey, Ali, Isla and Caleb, I am by far the luckiest aunty. The joy you kids bring me and our entire family is endless. All six of you have given life a new meaning, and Bobba would be so proud of you all. Wherever she is, she will always love you. Lee and Lauren, the support you have shown Greg and Ricky, and extended to Dad and me, has never gone unnoticed. I count myself very lucky to have you in my life.

Scottie, there are no words that can do justice to my gratitude to you. I have had the privilege of knowing you for almost ten years, and you have been my number-one fan, and I yours. Your belief in me is unconditional. When I told you I had scribbled some words down and I thought that one day I might write a book, you told me that it was to be. I would not be here, where I am today, without you. Thank you for believing in me and guiding me through the writing process. I know I always have a lot to say, but when it comes to you, I get lost for words, as words alone can't capture how grateful I am for you. Thank you, fave!

To Heidi, in you I found a confidante, a supporter, and one of the most extraordinary people I have ever met. You took me into the CHeBA family from the first day I contacted you and I am not going anywhere. Your support over the past ten years has been second to none. There is nothing you can't or won't do, and your commitment to CHeBA and every single one of us who has been affected by Alzheimer's shows such empathy, kindness and desire to make a difference. Thank you for setting up time with Dr Karen Mather and Professor Henry Brodaty to contribute important information and knowledge to this book. Thank you for the countless hours you spend on WipeOut Dementia, CHeBA Change Makers, running festivals and the million other things you do. You are one of a kind.

To Professor Henry Brodaty for generously making time to meet with me and contribute the important information regarding prevention and healthy brain ageing in this book, and pioneering CHeBA and the research that is paving the way for the future and is making a significant difference in the world of dementia. And to Dr Karen Mather who was so kind and patient in educating me on the important research she is undertaking and for contributing it to the book.

Ed and PJ, your passion, commitment, support and friendship never goes unnoticed. We connected through a shared experience of supporting our loved ones with Alzheimer's, and now we have truly become lifelong friends. Thank you for the hours you have spent listening to me talk about this book, and for your contributions. I know we are only getting started and I look forward to changing the world of Alzheimer's with you both.

Nick, Reidy and Anthony, thank you for sharing your stories with me and for so generously allowing me to tell them in this book. I know it wasn't easy and I only hope I can do your stories justice, as each one is so personal. The love and care you have shown towards your respective family members is to be admired.

Sheli, Kelly, Caz and Lynn, the time you spent with Mom will never be forgotten. I will be forever grateful for what you did for Mom and our family. We would not have gotten through it all without you. Thank you!

To my mom's brothers, thank you for always loving and taking care of your little sister – she was always adored and protected by you. And thank you for all the time you spent with her throughout her Alzheimer's journey.

To my extended Jankelowitz family, Mom was always so devoted to her cousins, nieces and nephews. She loved family more than anything. Thank you for the support and for spending time with Mom.

Paul, thank you for your delicacy and respect in editing this book. I had a lot to say, and thank you for helping me articulate it. It means so much to me that you were the one editing my story.

To the Hachette team, thank you for taking a chance on me and allowing me to tell my story. You have allowed me to fulfil a dream of helping others and bringing attention and awareness to dementia, and showing why we need to advocate for people who can't speak for themselves.

To Merv and Stan, I don't think you will ever know how much your support for Dad and our whole family has meant. The bond you three brothers have is undeniable. We always say, 'Granny and Oupa did something right,' because you three have paved the way for what it means to be a family. Thank you for the many phone calls and visits over the years and for helping us navigate some tricky situations. To Rose and Ev and all the Kitay cousins, no matter where we live in the world, your support and presence are always felt.

To the people who have been by my side all the way, thank you: Jonny Jon, Mossy, Dylz, Medders, Jus, Teen, Ash, Carls, Riks, Lis, Greeny, Ali, Lena, Coops, Tabs, Trac, Goob, Anna and everyone else – you know who you are.

I have been MIA this year, but your support and friendship over the years – in some cases, many years – means so much to me.

To every carer at the homes Mom lived in, thank you. You do the most selfless and thankless job in the world. You took care of Mom in the most trying of times, when my family and I couldn't care for her in the way she needed. No amount of thanks will ever be enough.

This may be my story, but this book is for every family out there experiencing dementia, and those who sadly will do so in the future. My promise to you is that I will make it my life's mission to advocate for our loved ones with dementia, to bring more awareness to our cause, and to help everyone navigate the process and push for better care, better systems and better access. I promise to ensure that your loved ones are humanised throughout their journeys, that they are always treated with empathy and respect.

To everyone going through a hard time navigating dementia or any type of disease, disability or illness, I see you and I am with you.

Lastly, to Mom, thank you for showing me what it means to lead with kindness, what a selfless life looks like and that the most important thing you can do in life is serve others. You taught me that what matters most is how you make people feel and how you treat others. You taught me the importance of being true to your values.

I promise to lead by your example. What I can't promise is that Dad and I will lose our warped sense of humour, and I will never forget the way you looked at us when you didn't approve of our laughter. It will forever be a favourite memory!

To the incredible people in my life, thank you. There are no words ...

Kindness always wins.